DISPATCHES FROM FI

Sarah Beddow's debut full-length collection, *Dispatches from Frontier Schools*, is an incredibly important contribution to our public discussions about education in the United States. Her testimony, these poems, makes evident the myriad and deeply troubling flaws in our public school system(s) and highlights all the ways students are dragged through schooling that serves no one by stressing expediency, rote memorization, and parroting over intellectual challenge and critical thinking: "A. is angry with me because / I made her read this book / and this conversation hurt / her / It hurts me / too," laments Beddow.

And behind their desks (and in their cars, and in their homes, grading papers late at night), Beddow shows us, again and again, that teachers are asked to hold an unsustainable amount of emotional, physical, and intellectual space for trends disguised as pedagogy, reactive administrative demands, and student needs that surpass the scope and breadth of K–12 training. These poems are brutal, laying bare the tragic and terrible ways our country is failing us all. But they are also full of moments that are often missing in contemporary education—like humility, compassion, and empathy: "we stand in the hallway as D. tells me / she is pregnant she is due in December She cries and covers her / face with her hands I well up but hide it by biting the inside of my bottom lip."

This book should be required reading for career administrators, board of education politicos, and all the legislators who pay little more than lip-service to our nation's educators. These poems—unique in structure and perspective, and full of beautifully orchestrated lyric turns—are a criticism, and a call for a reckoning, to be sure. "Wait I / I know this I remember /this This is burn/out The fire / out and in its place just / a rock lined pit," she writes in "Re: Gratitude." "the student who says thank you is rare You / are rare / And I look him in the eyes Then /I have to leave because soon this room will / be ablaze and I have nothing left to burn."

—**Sarah Kain Gutowski, author of** *Fabulous Beast: Poems*

In her memoir-in-poems *Dispatches from Frontier Schools*, Sarah Beddow creates a vital frontline record of American education as it abuts the pandemic. Here, we meet Beddow, a woman teacher in full, frank embodiment: an educator unwilling to subsume herself entirely to the twinned demands of capitalism and data-driven academic achievement bearing down on her and her students by her charter school employer, yet one who still burns to offer her entire intellectual and energetic self to her under-resourced students. "In the Instruction and Culture Cabinet meeting I once again / melted / when the principal asked us to be a team," she writes in the poem "Dispatch re: White Out," "to / buy in I buy in / I always / buy in . . . in the end when I arrive home I don't talk to my / family like I've been thinking / to and instead / I write about the day / about the exhaustion / about the students we do not serve." Throughout *Dispatches from Frontier Schools*, Beddow contrasts the sterile and un-seeing language of corporate education with her own vibrant, devastating personal testimonies and disclosures, granting us an intimate, eviscerating glimpse into the negotiations, struggles, heartbreaks, and joys as lived from her side of the overflowing teacher's desk.

—**Rachel Mennies, author of** *The Naomi Letters*

Sarah Beddow's bullshit detector is razor-sharp. Her *Dispatches from Frontier Schools* exposes what's wrong with K–12 education in the United States: a corporate profit model infiltrating what should be a free public good where the only players the executives value less than the teachers are the students themselves.

High school students are built out of bullshit and swagger, which adults can anticipate. Beddow writes, "Mind your business / they say   Sweet girls haven't you realized You / are / my business." What we should not have to anticipate is bad behavior from fellow adults in the workplace. Bad colleagues make a hard job impossible. "He then played a game of / keep away with the paper / over the staff lounge table." The students will break your heart, but the administrators will crush it.

These Dispatches unsparingly critique not just the institution, but the complicity of every adult working within it, including Ms. Beddow the teacher, who sometimes yells or slams a door. "I listened to my ideas   come out of his mouth my own mouth / muted / And it's like   I am not here I am / divorced from my / thoughts I am told again and again to join the / team." An institution with incompetent management can tank the best teachers, run the best future leaders out the door. "But no amount of reflection   will reveal to me how   to be / professional in a system   so broken it / shreds me   leaves me a corpse in underwear and an ancient / t-shirt   spread / on the classroom floor." This book is for anyone concerned about the future.

—**Krystal Languell, author of** *Systems Thinking with Flowers*

DISPATCHES FROM FRONTIER SCHOOLS

Sarah Beddow

Riot in Your Throat
publishing fierce, feminist poetry

Beddow, Sarah.
1st edition.
ISBN: 978-1-7361386-5-6

Cover Photo: Sarah Beddow
Cover Design: Kirsten Birst
Book Design: Shanna Compton
Author Photo: Sarah Beddow

Riot in Your Throat
Arlington, VA
www.riotinyourthroat.com

For the senior team, in all its permutations. For all the teachers, all the counselors, and all the staff at the real-life Frontier Schools. I see you. I appreciate you. Shout out to you.

CONTENTS

YEAR THREE

YEAR FOUR

YEAR FIVE

i loved you on purpose
i was open on purpose

—Ntozake Shange

It's evident
the art of losing's not too hard to master
though it may look like (Write it!) like disaster.

—Elizabeth Bishop

DISPATCH
re: You

> *The Wolf saw him coming towards her, pale and wild-eyed, with the axe gleaming in the sun, and did not retreat a single step, did not lower her eyes, but continued to walk toward him, with her hands full of red poppies . . .*
> —Giovanni Verga

I first learned to teach   /   in jail   and then I taught Sarah Lawrence undergraduates how to teach /   in jail   If you are a teacher you can /   already guess who was harder to   wrangle   If you   /   are not a teacher   Let me tell you about the school secretaries from /   when I was subbing in the suburbs   I showed up /   early   and /   most made small talk   Some inexplicably treated me /   like a nuisance But whenever I said I had just moved home from New York   that I had been /   teaching in the Bronx   those women to a one   /   ooohed and awed over my saintliness for teaching /   those   /   children   living /   there   /   That must have been /   so   /   hard   The school was eight stories high   with four thousand students on roster and a little over two thousand showing up daily /   on a good day   I worked hard to develop ways to /   humanize my students   in /   a sentence or two   for these secretaries   You should have /   seen them in their prom gowns and tuxes   I'd say or   /   more often   / Oh no   they're just   kids Just kids   / It wasn't a /   thing   But it was   /   most definitely   a thing   I /   cried   all the time   My friends   /   quit or were   fired /   every year The kids   sometimes /   dropped out and I only knew because one / day they stopped coming and a few /   weeks after that   their names would disappear   from /   the Scantron rosters   What /   would it have looked like /   instead   /   to   humanize myself   If you are a teacher /   you know   this   double/bind   If you are not   /   a teacher   let me

tell you about Carlos who drew me a gift an anthropomorphized
sexy wolf woman with / a crop top and pointy / ears and / long
sharp teeth He labeled it "The Wolf" after the main character of
"The Wolf" by Giovanni Verga which we / were reading together
The drawing is pencil on notebook paper / it has been punctured
by   multiple push pins Almost all I have left of those years /
anymore is a question Which of us was the wolf with hands full
of bloodred flowers which the desperate man / with the axe

YEAR ONE

DISPATCH
re: Hope

In my classroom today I saw a kid / put his fingers up in a vee against / his mouth / and wriggle his red tongue across / the room / toward me but not / for / me   Then he refused to look / at / me I saw it I saw you / insert yourself into a woman's space into her / right to learn   / this is an artificial matriarchal space / sings eunsong on twitter / birdsong necessary to life in sub/urban spaces   But how do I / make a matriarchal space in the class / room   When I was in middle school a tiny / folded note was passed around the circle of desks / in German class / inevertellthisstory and shit i tell all the stories especially the shocking ones over and / over / and when it got to me i opened it and a few generous pinches of pubic hairs fell all over my desk and my lap and my fingers touched them and they stuck to me and / i / was the one who was ashamed / cheeks on fire across the room fucking Denny and / who / probably Josh laughed and laughed Still i do not know / if that note was aimed at me or if i was just innocent / unlucky / naive the one who opened it and hoped / for more

DISPATCH

for: [redacted]

I do not do / emotions / well   I am stoic and disinclined to touch
when upset When doctors cut my dead baby from my body / I woke
up alone in a crowded recovery room   shivering and crying and   /
even if my husband had been there   I didn't want / to be touched
What would have happened /   I would have   cried myself   into /
dissolution [Redacted] came to me during my prep to get something
off her chest and she only cried for / a few seconds   the whole
period   / We talked about what / she owed her friend

        /

                          /
/   now that they   share /
                  the manifold /   /
                   I do not want
              I do not want   do not want cannot
stand this world / for them So I touched / her and listened She did
not dissolve   today but / surely she will / and / if I can I will be the
nurse who notices   the silent shivering the silent tears   and brings
an extra blanket

DISPATCH
re: Monday's Bomb Threat

> *For something sufficiently toad-like*
> *Squats in me, too;*
> *Its hunkers are heavy as hard luck,*
> *And cold as snow . . .*
> —Philip Larkin

There are nights I want to write but I do not write because I do not do / anything on those nights but drink and struggle to stay / awake till 8:30 when I wash my face then pass out / heavy   I feel / little   save the toad squatting on / my life on my chest This physical pressure / that I cannot drive off Tonight I wept / while watching *Call the Midwife* snuggling on my son's / soft / blue Jojo The soap that ran into my mouth / when I washed my face / tasted like salt A student who wrote a love poem recalling Breton / *her legs like tons of boiled noodles in water* / told me he isn't coming back next year   His parents want him to go back to his home district a district so sunk into   failure he can't / go back there because they're shuttering the high school and busing the few hundred remaining / students to the district next   door We had a bomb threat on Monday the whole school stood in the cold rain for / two hours I am so / shallow I only cared that the rain was gonna ruin / my / purple shoes these purple Fluevogs that I coveted for years before finally / buying them for myself a few weeks ago The K-9 unit covered entry / two mornings this week because of a / gun threat / written on a bathroom stall No one believed / either threat was sincere   But this / is a school where just a year ago a student / did / bring a gun to school /   Lockdown is in / everyone's   working vocabulary I have no vocabulary / to spell out the difference between what my brain knows to be true / and

how this feels / to the toad   in my heart / Larkin   had not one
toad   but two / *I don't say one   bodies   the other one's spiritual truth*
/ he said   But my body   my spirit   this job   all hunker / heavy
and   cold   a / single   brute force   I cannot   throw   off

DISPATCH
re: Compliance

.

This morning I considered the advantages of finally crying / in the Giant Eagle parking lot Catharsis   even over donuts is still / cathartic But there were / no donuts / I promised my best class my most engaged students a donut party and how / can there be no donuts at 6:30 in the morning / When else would I eat donuts than in the fluorescent morning / before sunrise   / on another Friday so desperate because there is   no weekend / anymore / just two sequential 12-hour days of / planning   and grading Our sister high school visited our classrooms last week to / evaluate / student engagement / The teachers who visited me and Ms. Long   ranked our class our donut winning class just / Compliant / They graded / me / with a / slap Not a single teacher checked / Highly Engaged / I welcomed these teachers / to our room with extra copies of handouts and / chitchat that does not come easy to me / The classroom was full of students deconstructing Jessica Williams' argument about Beyoncé at the Super Bowl   reading Marxist critiques of Beyoncé formulating original arguments about Beyoncé's surprise turn   to Black Lives Matter If / this / is compliance then / I do not know why / why I am an   absent mother / failing wife / fat ass with a muffin top I have / nothing else / to give no ideas better than these / no students more woke / no donuts / no tears left to cry in the parking lot dawn / no   me

DISPATCH

re: Beyoncé

> *I see it, I want it, I stunt, yellow-bone it*
> *I dream it, I work hard, I grind 'til I own it*
> *I twirl on my haters, albino alligators*
> —Beyoncé, "Formation"

Today we talked in circles / Good / circles around the (imaginary) seminar table around Beyoncé's / intentions and effects with "Formation"   around the revolution / and capitalism and if ever the twain will / meet   J.   said with a / shit-eating grin that if he were president he would stop all women from voting / And the class laughed / I / stepped into the student-centered seminar space and shut / that / down I stopped a girl from laughing so I / could protect my own space / my own / comfort in my / classroom to clarify that disenfranchising women comes from a place of / hatred that proposing stripping / half the population of their right to vote / because of their sex / was not funny It was shocking to hear a young / man so confidently / propose denying women / human rights And that ever-green rebuttal / But this / is an open space to talk / I am / just / voicing my opinion / And my ever-green response Your / right to speech does not / free   you   from criticism / And some opinions / are / wrong   J. waved me off to / save face But I won   What does it mean to /   defeat a student Do I continue / to grind continue / to twirl or just pretend that I think he wasn't / serious   Oh he was To him / I am less than / human I suppose so is /   Beyoncé And so are half his classmates /   But they   find him funny

DISPATCH
re: Labor

I remember the rules, rules that were never spelled out but every woman knew: Don't open your door to a stranger, even if he says he is the police. Make him slide his ID under the door. Don't stop on the road to help a motorist pretending to be in trouble. Keep the locks on and keep going. If anyone whistles, don't turn to look.
—Margaret Atwood

Janese Talton-Jackson was shot in Homewood a twenty minute drive from / where I work It happened just a month ago while I was teaching / *The Handmaid's Tale*   and the parallels were clear / are clear She said / No / to the man/ but No was a violation   The man / shot her in the chest This country is deliriously / close to Gilead For what balm is there   A better option than / the alternative   on the surface / but is this /   trading one dystopia / for another   This school where it smells like / teenage flop sweat teacher / flop sweat Where the teachers call off because they are / extended beyond their limits and it's / only / March But the district   tells us / Do Not Use Your Days You Will Be Paid Out in September We know we / will be paid out at / a fraction of our salaried rate because we are just / worn cogs in a machine for making   a nonprofit   profitable Did you know our school has / investors / They are not the parents not the students They are stakeholders who look at our / numbers We are numbers and data and a rung on someone else's ladder / Someone more patriarchal more / driven   I said to Principal Osborne when he gave me a third course / Three courses will break me / and here / I am breaking because this course load is too much this school is too broken / Why does no one hear us when we say we cannot we cannot carry this load The cost / of saying No is   white lies and   white guilt and fear of dismissal   After / reading Janese Talton-Jackson's story in class a student asked me how / a woman can ever say / No / He couldn't even figure out how / to ask the question but he wanted to know   to fix the problem to be anything but the problem / and all I could tell him was It is hard it takes / energy to   balance your need to say No with a man's need to be in control / What could a woman do I asked him / with all that mental energy she spends following the rules   /   appeasing a man's will   What wonderful things / she could think / then

DISPATCH

re: Divestment

I told our new School Resource Officer that I had to / divest myself of whiteness / in jest but also / it is no joke   Teaching Ta-Nehisi Coates to an integrated classroom / to a 75% Black classroom / is hard   Coates writes essays that make meaning like / poems and my students / struggle to / leap from slavery to   the Dream   to the Mecca / In our Socratic seminar   one student / excels on the rubric   A. asks questions   she / challenges her classmates when their assumptions are / easy   A. is white / and fragile   She / raises her hand   questions why we can't all just get along   / contends that Coates' writing about slavery is / opening up old wounds / She leaps / easily between slavery   violence   the Dream the police   She falls / in the   leap back into her own / white skin   She / is not racist / She should not have to read / Coates' visceral / fact-based / pain cry   We should all / move on / But my job is not to tell her what to think / My job is to open her eyes / My job / is / to tell her what to think / My job is to encourage her challenges and questions / My job is to create safe   spaces for   my Black students / her friends / Keep them   from having to explain / again and again / that racism is real and present   That / A. will / get a job more easily / than V. who has higher grades   the greater / work ethic   That she will not fear violence / when she is stopped by a cop / Like J. and W. did when our very SRO pulled them / over   a few months for no reason / My job is / not to protect students who are / capable of protecting / themselves   Now A. is angry with me because / I made her read this book / and this conversation hurt / her /   It hurts me / too   On the kitchen counter / at home / lay the papers that will send my son to a / good / suburban school   for kindergarten in the fall   A / good / suburban school   where the student / body is overwhelmingly white and / model minority / is 98% proficient in Math and English / is overwhelmingly college-bound where / I / went where / I / learned to challenge to question to write my name / in cursive to celebrate my / dominance in the classroom

DISPATCH
re: the Bar

This is a night out   for me for my husband and it is cold and rainy
I am dressed in my green leather jacket and perfect black witch shoes
/ that is what my daughter   Willa calls them / Witch Shoes / There
are no tables available until / 10:30 I stand behind various people at
the bar / awkward / hoping but I will not cry here in the restaurant
for my birthday   In yesterday's discussion of *For Colored Girls* D.
asked her classmates   Wouldn't it be / nice if women just did   what
we were / supposed to / / for once   and all these hands shot into the
air / desperate My own hand   shot in the air   My husband / makes
more than me   by a lot   but works / far fewer hours / and from
home He / does the dishes takes the kids to preschool shops / for
groceries makes dinner   packs my lunch   makes my   / breakfast
Still / when preschool moms email about the next birthday party
they email / me and I fuck it up because I have no time to read my
email until the weekend   when the RSVP date has passed and
there is another email asking if I could please RSVP /   already /
because I / must be a terrible mom Am I doing what I'm / supposed
to / teaching   other people's children about the social construction
of gender why / rape is not a woman's fault   how / a vagina does
not make a lady especially   good / at vacuuming the stairs I see
/ now what I need to do better in my / classroom   Make room for
discomfort   and the student who just / doesn't fit   The woman
sitting / in the bar stool in front of us leans back and tells me We're
about / to leave Do you want these seats Here have / a menu I wish I
had known / there was this special where you can get the Mexican
street corn but with / crab on top too

DISPATCH
re: Ice in April

The roads this morning were treacherous / with ice and why even / write this The metaphors are obvious I'm / cold I'm on / thin ice I'm risking my / health my life / for this job / The fifth of April and the roads are covered / in ice Twice I lost control of the car When I pulled into the school / driveway I sobbed and sobbed I wished more than once I / had / crashed Then I'd be / excused First period had already begun and / K. and T. had been burying their noses in their phones had been ignoring their work had been / belittling me / for days I cried / more in the bathroom I / had to go back into / that room no space / between their drama and the ice that melted miles before I arrived at school / making me seem a drama queen a fraud / When I was in high school my friends talked about me / in the locker room made lists / of dudes I screwed but I was still / a virgin Sure I sucked boys off but those boys were smart and didn't / tell Still / somehow / those girls knew / about me K. and T. don't know / about me but still / somehow they do Back then there were no cell phones no / texts no / high-speed dramas that sucked us away from / here and now Now / I have nothing but / here and now / the walls surrounding me the numbing ice

DISPATCH
re: my Love

> *my love is too delicate to have thrown back on my face*
> *my love is too beautiful to have thrown back on my face*
> *my love is too magic to have thrown back on my face*
> —Ntozake Shange

K. and T. are fighting in first   period   /   again   But this time with another student   N. /   flared   against a discussion of rape culture   Females have /   all the power he said   Females can say / no anytime   You have the power   /   of denial he says and all we / have are   blueballs K. and T. look at him with / shock   mouths gaping for a few long   seconds   /   I am used to / students who try to shock me   And I've heard this idea   before Unfortunately I have no / effective rhetorical   counter beyond   Are you /   damaged so I let it /   play out   I wonder /   privately   if this conception of the / power of denial   is related to body counts   How / my body count is too high   how any girl with any body / count at all   is a thot The kids / taught me that   word   To /   experience pleasure is to / cede your power All that power we have /   nowhere to spend it   No room in this formulation for / love either It turns out / I was right to let / it ride   K. hits play on her computer   and Thandiwe Newton reads / from *For Colored Girls*   My love is too delicate / to have thrown back on my face   My love is too beautiful to have / thrown back on my face   K. and T. smile smugly   point at the screen   recite along with the track   My love is too / magic   to have thrown back on my face   N. rolls his eyes   the girls / return to their   analysis They still hate me   I think / I still hate them even though inside /   a small bud of joy   opens a millimeter   two Today   my love   was too / beautiful   to throw back in my face

DISPATCH
re: Shadows

These students do   not   leave my room   There are no prep periods I have / no time without kids   talking   writing   talking talking talk/ ing / ing / ing My job is to / control the room   keep everyone on task / proofread this paper / provide followable advice on how to completely restructure that paper / sit hold space for D. at my elbow while she types her paper and types types   types / The skylight points sun at my eyes at a 45 degree / angle and I'm wearing this cowgirl hat from my days as a cook at Tara Mandala   to stop the daily headache from bleeding into / tomorrow and tomorrow and tomorrow / At home I take the hat off but still / hide my eyes   I can't look at my kids I can't make eye contact with / anyone   My husband   says it's OK I'm / always like this after work / I'm always like this / I think I could fall asleep / on this hard plastic chair here / in the sunshine   of the back yard   My kids climb the swingset and slide   slide / The shadows grow long like shadows do in late Spring   / I move my chair back and back / to keep my body warm in the sun / shine farther away and farther / away from my   kids until there is nothing left but shadows

DISPATCH
re: Giant Eagle Cupcake Cake

This time last year   I was a substitute teacher with / no school to call / home / I intruded by request and left as little evidence of / myself / as possible One day when I was / a subbing   9th-grade English the afternoon was an assembly   a dress rehearsal / for the musical I sat alone   useless because even if / a kid misbehaved I knew / no one's name   had no / power   The overture began   the Cat in the Hat rhymed frantically on stage   and / through the back doors of the auditorium burst the rest of the cast / singing / singing I couldn't / I sobbed and stifled it   Today / I watched the lip sync at our Advisory Olympics felt the same surge tenderness / grief   push up my throat and / blur my sight / We sat around the table in the breakroom a few hours / later   discussing the kids who / simply cannot pass / who are not capable of meeting the standard who need / so much help and / care / We ate a cake made of cupcakes / shaped like an ice cream cone / We dipped our fingers into the piles of supermarket frosting   First me / then our guidance counselor   then Principal Osborne then / me then   Ms. Long   The sugar / the fat / it was too much / so sweet / I ate till I gagged I   stifled it I didn't turn / away / I ate more and more shoving / sugar down my throat because Giant Eagle cake will never taste like anything / but home

DISPATCH
re: Graduation

I am / devastated stuck in brutal traffic   Late for the ceremony
This morning I was / humiliated by parents   / by Osborne and
/ perhaps worst / by S.   who sat in my room two days ago / so
high   he was unable to / finish his work   to pass my class / to
graduate Work which was due / a month ago S.   let his parents
yell at me like / I was incompetent like he hadn't received Fs / on
each and every report card this / year like we hadn't all sat in   a
parent/teacher conference six weeks ago / Osborne   swooped in
/ principal/hero / advocated for him / plead that he deserved a
second chance when I argued for failure I even said / to Osborne
/ I am not comfortable with the decision / I said But what can I do
I put my / powerlessness in his face and he accepted it as his due
right I said / You know this was his / fifth / chance Then Osborne
/ smiled and   changed / the grade   The speaker tonight is a Black
man who   knows how to work a crowd and terrify / kindly white
teachers and administrators   / He tells a story about a / miracle /
how he broke so many laws   /   killed people in his life / but the
one time he was arrested / he didn't / do it So he got off / Didn't
say I was innocent said I didn't do / that / And the crowd in the
hall roared   and the administrators on stage sat / statuesque with
heads turned to the left and right ankles   crossed / demurely over
left His story went on / and his inspirational message / to students
on the edge of / adulthood / was   It / doesn't / matter   what you
did what happened in the past The future is / yours And I cry
/ again / because   the future / is / theirs I want only love /   and
success for them   But / it does /   it does matter   It has to matter
that I was humiliated so S. / could sit here / be absolved / by this
inspirational speaker So he could   walk happily up the hill after the
ceremony / avoid my eyes /   run into his   future

DISPATCH
re: End of Year Party

> *And for so long I have wanted to escape into the Dream,*
> *to fold my country over my head like a blanket. But*
> *this has never been an option because the Dream rests*
> *on our backs, the bedding made from our bodies.*
> —Ta-Nehisi Coates

In the beer garden with white sailor hats because / one of our
team building activities was to / decorate sailor hats The music is
entirely / white Pittsburgh nothing but / The Eagles The Stones
Steve Miller Band The Dead CCR The / Who And I pause / for
a moment / Even this 11am crowd of / burned out teachers / in all
our womanity all we get is / the culture of white men Later / at
lunch / as I turn from white to bright red in the midday sun of
mid June / I argue with Hayes about whiteness / A white man he
does not believe / Ta-Nehisi Coates got his own / story right and
I have been drinking for hours already / so I bite You can disagree
with his conclusions / I am still teaching / but you cannot tell
him his experiences / are false This / is the English 12 rule of
Socratic seminars / Hayes does not get it is / drunk too Coates
could change / his story if only / he wanted to The Dream
/ is for all of us / America the beautiful and some shit When I
say next that / my / identity too deeply informs / my / life he
snortles through some beer I can say those things others think but
don't / voice aloud I explain because I am small and blonde I
am pretty in the face I can swear a hot streak call my boss an
idiot / in so many words / and all I get is / plaudits Hayes says /
Who said you're pretty / Oh haha white man as if every man
I've ever known like you hasn't told me so / in as many ways as

he can figure   / from his hands all over me   to his eyes all over me
to his   / requests for my time when   I am busy   to his requests for
my time   / when I am disinterested   To his   body naked   / in my
bed   when I'm   thirsty   I drink / more beer   I would not / be me
without this face   this /   white skin   this / compact body   This
body now   drunk   and tired of / careful   elisions   and   snickering
eye rolls   In the car ride home / of course   Moby   on the radio /
making his fortune   even these fifteen years later   appropriating
Black voices   I used to fuck /   to Moby who knows how many times
/ Body on fire   and body / soaked   in the comedown   White body
lying / by white body   Hearing   but / not hearing the voices   The
Dream   subsumed in   our   wantonness and / sleep

YEAR TWO

DISPATCH
re: First Day of Kindergarten

With my group of ten advisory students we held / a funeral for all
our can'ts I can't / sing   You can't / do math You'll never lose
those man-tits I can't be a good / mom and a good teacher We
buried them in a shoebox said words over the box / Stomped it in a
/ frenzy of violence and threw it in the dumpster out back / behind
the loading dock / Cooking on the blacktop of late August   I left
those kids / behind today to stand at the bus stop with my kid / who
is five and starting kindergarten The bus didn't come   didn't
come   the baby waiting with her older sister started to cry   Our
neighbors' kids   hit each other / We called the school Yes yes we're
sorry All the buses are / running late / Until a parent from the bus
stop up the street drove by with her daughter because she gave / up
and another parent drove / past the other way looking looking /
searching anywhere for a bus that should have come an hour ago
/ We drove Emmett to school He was late and the teacher / nearly
slammed the door behind him I never said / goodbye I didn't say I
love you Good luck you are / amazing And he was gone and my
morning was wasted because I didn't get a picture of him boarding
his bus for the first time / and I can't stay home / tomorrow again / I
can't leave these / other kids who / need me I can't take a / picture
to show them the back of Emmett's head walking up / the black
stairs of the school bus climbing / without a backwards glance

DISPATCH
re: Gun Day

Gun Day   is a proper noun here   I wasn't / around for Gun Day
it was two years / ago midyear   A gun was found in the parking
lot and protocol   said / search for a second gun if ever a first / is
found They found a second / gun inside Today is training day
what to do if Gun Day recurs / To train   we listen to the 911 call
from Columbine High School   tracked over the security camera
footage of kids running / The call is long 10 minutes   20 minutes
/ 30 minutes The whole time kids / killing kids / and no adult
comes into the building   / to stop them / After Gun Day / Mrs.
Carroll bought a gun She said she / never would buy a gun / good
liberal and all I am / ungenerous / I bet it's a pink fucking gun like
those hammers and screwdrivers that come in Laura Ashley flowers
so women / will buy them   Mrs. Carroll bought / a gun after
spending a day locked in a room / with her students while cops /
searched the building But she still doesn't know / how to use it /
Years ago NPR reported on a new law allowing teachers to conceal
and carry / The woman on the phone   a teacher / was confident
carrying her gun   / into the classroom She knew / don't have a
gun if you cannot / will not use it When asked she confirmed
/ Yes / I will   shoot a student / if he is threatening / Shoot a
student she would shoot / a student she would shoot / I cannot
predict the future but / I will never buy a gun / I will   / never
/ own a gun / During the training Ms. Miller asks what to do
if the students do not / comply with police   orders during a Gun
Day This is a good / question They do not trust the police They
will not / comply And they are right This is wrong   Someone
will / shoot

DISPATCH
re: the Definition of

My room this year has two / teacher desks My student teacher has /
festooned hers with a banner of tiny pennants and a fake plastic /
plant from Ikea In the houseplant she has tucked tightly wound /
scrolls of paper with / prompts for charades She thinks you can
define feminism / without using the word woman and I get it
but / also I refuse the elision In class / we use my definition /
not hers But I nod at it / respectfully Today in advisory / she
has the students in a tight circle They have written definitions of
/ crime / on notecards For each definition they / share she asks
them another question pushing / them deeper Crime is breaking
the laws What / is a law she / asks A law is a rule about what
not to do but with like official punishments Who enforces / that
rule she asks / The government enforces the rules Well / what
did the government base those rules on / she asks This one stumps
them / But D. says What's right and what's wrong My student
teacher is / into it now But who decides what's right / and
what's wrong E. supplies I guess we do with a question mark /
turning up her voice at the end Oh why is it a question she asks /
grabbing a whiteboard marker Do you think maybe / we / don't
decide She is so / excited she only waves her arms and forgets about
/ writing on the whiteboard Who else could it be who / decides
right from wrong I watch them all / from the back of the room
I can see / where she is going but they / don't / not yet anyway
They are moments from seeing / from being guided to a definition
of / we / that is not them Or perhaps they do / see where
she is coming from Perhaps they refuse / the elision

DISPATCH
re: my Teeth

There is a black spot between / my molars on the bottom right-hand side Investigating that black spot I saw another small spot on the side of my molar where the enamel is gone / gone and left behind is a perfectly / circular sensitive spot so I don't touch it / or think about it / I think about it all the time Is this where my son / got his nutrients / while nursing / while I ate so very little food / because he was allergic to everything / but probably he wasn't That was just what the nutritionist guessed / I didn't eat / dairy wheat soy egg chocolate sugar gluten booze Ha / I kid / I still drank I tell my students this / That a mother's body is so dedicated to her baby she will cannibalize herself She could be near starving and her teeth will fall to pieces but the baby will have strong / bones

DISPATCH
re: *Satan at Our Backs*

i waz missin somethin
somethin so important
somethin promised
a layin on of hands
fingers near my forehead
strong
cool
movin
makin me whole
    —Ntozake Shange

Ms. Katz said that her massage therapist / told her that her mother
was sitting on her / shoulders My students sit / on my neck and
ride my / jaw If someone could just / touch me maybe drive her
fingers deep into the tissue those / students would get behind
me When this year / started I posted a link to an essay on the rise
/ in witchcraft among millennials / I posted the link to say that
the essay led me to epiphany I / needed / to plan my desk my
knickknacks my pens my art my lamp because I was building /
an altar To protect myself from the needs needs needs of my /
students And my mom told me to reframe / it's not productive / for
the students to find in me a brick wall I should / police myself
and my needs because / my needs are / bad for my students I love
them on purpose I am / open on purpose I reach out / let
them hug me / or hold my hand Touch them on the shoulder / to
say good job / to say / are you on / task Positive touch and it may
be technically illegal or unethical / a union would never / defend
me for touching a student but how else / to make ourselves whole

DISPATCH

re: Comments on Timed Essays about "It's a Woman's World"
by Eavan Boland

> *Appearances reassure . . .*
> *While this one here,*
> *her mouth a burning plume—*
>
> *she's no fire-eater,*
> *just my frosty neighbour*
> *coming home.*
> —Eavan Boland

Yes   women are stuck behind the scenes But / does Boland think
they really do / nothing / back there Anchor this / observation to
the washing powder / the forgotten loaf etc If we have forgotten
women have strength / power / muscle mass / desire   then what is
the woman thinking of when / she forgets / again / to finish her
chores tidy the house / put a balanced meal on the table   I   / will
buy / your claim that the / women's world / of the title is where
the irony / lies but I still wonder / what about that alibi   What
about / those / women who weren't   at the scene of the crime   /
why mention the crime just to alibi / out the women   Definitely
your strongest / essay yet You got the 90%   now / can you learn to
grab that last 10% Just / you cannot retitle the poem / It's a Man's
World / without losing / the power of the work There is no / king's
world / This / is not a king's world Again / what if the title isn't the
irony   Even though you told me you didn't / get this poem at all
I think / you actually understood a lot But I'd challenge whether
Boland believes women / are / going nowhere You yourself pointed
out / that women birthed the world Boland / believes / in our
power / You're right / it is ironic / that the woman who lives by

the hearth / is no fire-eater But if she forgot / the loaf at the register / what else is there to eat / this night / but fire

DISPATCH
re: Critical Thinking

Please know that I am not one / to hold back I say what the room is thinking I say it / smart and fast / funny / dirty I've spent a lifetime mortifying my brother with my body My blood / my masturbation habits / my queries about the inevitability of queefing after doggy style / These were toothless attacks provocations / only / they were also / are also / my truth   My dad told me / of course my brother stood no chance / in a fight with me / If the bar for entry is knowing things / and having control of the language He was a goner But then why am I / the bitch when he started it / And my prowess as a debater as an academic as the smartest cunt in the room / precedes me especially within my / family Should I have told him / Yes / sweetie / critical thought / Good conclusion You're so / wise and let him walk all over my body / excused his refusal to vote refusal to save / my right to control / my / body my daughter's right to control / her / body my students' rights to control / their / bodies my student's body on a registry for Muslims Should I have muzzled the heart of myself / my heart of words and fire / to save his / ego My brother has / never had to worry about anyone / regulating his body without / his / consent / because that doesn't happen to cis straight white boys in the suburbs Does he know does he not / realize that I am paid to have these conversations / am expert in poking holes in students' thinking driving them back to the evidence / to support to / refine their arguments This is my / body poking holes in your arguments / My toothy body chewing your rhetoric to chum My / vagina dentata sucking up your hot air / to blow it out my vag

DISPATCH
re: Shit To Do

I have been working since 6:50 It is   now   6:49   / I reflected on
why I am a good educator for two hours tonight because what I
was allowed to do on my eval form last time / finish it later because
Osborne wouldn't look at it till later / I wasn't allowed to do this
time When Assistant Principal Cosentino told me to finish it the
toad in my chest / retreated beneath / the scum and I did yoga /
just so I could get to drinking wine time Last week / I made waffles
for 70 students and teachers / does that make me a good educator
This week / I will make banana bread with buttermilk and lots of
sugar for the student teachers so I can be / a good educator I am
making / my / student teacher a care package with B12 tablets   a
Do-or-Die notepad   her favorite / pens which are not my favorite
pens but / I am observant so I know what she needs / which is not
a planner though dear god / she needs a planner but I know / she
will not use it I made oatmeal raisin cookies for Ms. Long   for
her birthday and every week / I / update the STD board in the
staff lounge with our collective Shit To Do / the never-ending list of
Google forms and / phone calls and staff satisfaction surveys / So I
can be a good educator / I listened to Tori in the car this morning
and I think that is not healthy / to listen to Tori asking why / do / we
crucify ourselves   / because that is hyperbolic / really

DISPATCH
re: Car Speakers

> *Pitty, pitty, pitty pat*
> *Why you always doing that?*
> *Why you always talking smack?*
> —Grimes and Janelle Monáe, "Venus Fly"

Skip skip <u>play</u> Why you looking at me   Why / you / looking at me / now / Louder and more / all the drive home / <u>Repeat</u>   And no one / looks at me / <u>Repeat</u> / No one looks at me in fourth / period either   Usually they look at me / in advisory but today / D. talked about a creepy customer she had to help at Footlocker   and how she buzzed Q. over and over and over to come up and get the guy to go away   How / important / as a girl   to have a boy who knows   and will bounce assholes   When I waited tables there was one / man who touched me   a lot / on the waist / <u>Repeat</u> / the arm   again his arm around my waist   I / refused to wait on him   Well / I refused after my manager suggested   that guy was a creep   and why not / just avoid him   Let / my manager   wait the table when this   dick came / in   I tried to tell this story   to D. and Q.   to explain / how to protect yourself   as a woman in a public space   / to tell Q. about his responsibilities as a   man   who understands   But they didn't see me / <u>Repeat</u> / after I listened to their story   In fourth period / it's mean girls / talking when I ask them not to / talking when I sit on their table / my ass inches from their talking / talking / talking mouths and faces / Why you always talking / smack   No one looks at me / <u>Repeat</u> /Driving home I say it   Drivers can't hear me   don't see me   Fuck you   stay / in your lane / <u>Repeat</u> / And bitch if you are in my room / I will   as Ntozake says *tell all yr secrets bout yourself to yr face*   Your faces / in my room   turned from me   I am not invisible

/ I am body filled with / feelings   history of touch / I pound on
the / feelings with bass from blown car speakers Why you looking
at <u>Repeat</u> me / the mean girls ask Mind your business / they say
Sweet girls haven't you realized   You / are / my business

DISPATCH
re: Gratitude

AP Cosentino sits in for my mid-year evaluation My students like me and they know / how to perform for admin asking clarifying questions and   restating / a peer's comments before building on them with a / new but related insight But I fuck the timing all up This was two lessons / not one The feeling of failure sits / hunkers like hard luck I know in my brain / I was awesome I was / on fire / But the toad is cold and he has / moved in / Wait I / I know this I remember / this This is burn/out The fire / out and in its place just / a rock lined pit Now it is 3:15   Friday afternoon I am asleep on my feet I am still at work / I've been in meetings and conferences since 6:45 Just a / 23-minute lunch / Finally this meeting with T.   and his mom and his eight / teachers ends T. thanks us He says I just want to thank you all You have / my gratitude   He is sitting next to me   hiding his eyes /   I feel the gratitude roll off him in waves / It sweeps the room   settles into the pit   inside me I tell him   That thing you just did   when you thanked us The student who says   thank you is rare You / are rare / And I look him in the eyes Then / I have to leave   because soon   this room will / be ablaze and I have nothing left to burn

DISPATCH
re: Sex Dream

Sitting on the table outside my door at 7:35 doing / hall duty and grading I see / B. who always gives me a hard time / in eighth period putting his jacket / in his locker and feel the dream I had about him / the night before I was in my bedroom but my bedroom was an art classroom in a building with spiraling ramps around the outside / Three Rivers Stadium perhaps / My husband was reading a love letter I wrote / to provide constructive feedback I placed it in the paint-splattered sink for safekeeping among jugs of water and brushes My husband took our daughter to give / me space Dream B. appeared Then he was shirtless and so / skinny his chest was concave I held him / grasped at him so fiercely devoured him fucked / him in a way I only / fucked when I was much younger and unworldly I cannot / look at him in the here and now / I make notes / on my clipboard instead One of the comics I teach / in Creative Writing is a series of vignettes about / the artist's dad Many are dreams In one the dad is on his deathbed but then the dad and son are swimming The father holds / his son in the water expresses his / love and the son gets / an erection Last year students / exclaimed Oh that's wrong and I / wondered if I should redact / the comic or remove it from / the anthology entirely But instead I left it there / as is I try to explain when they / protest that dreams are symbolic The erection isn't an erection It's a physical manifestation of the invisible / It's the drive to connect reach out / hold on to love

DISPATCH
re: Paolo Freire

The central problem is this: How can the oppressed, as divided, unauthentic beings, participate in developing the pedagogy of their liberation?
—Paolo Freire

That's ignorant / that's ignorant to give us a final paper when we have our senior seminar paper due / It's ignorant to ask students to / excel to prove / they have learned to ask them to write / in English class All I want is time / to write / A quiet room / of my own Space and prompts and a critical audience to help me square my role as a teacher with my life as a / mother to line up my dictatorial / ignorant / assignments with a liberation pedagogy based on what / students already know / My student teacher's lessons lack / focus deliberation She knows this / but she cannot fix it She worships at the altar / of Freire My old grad school papers / written in my old classroom during prep periods / reveal I have always had practical questions about the / praxis of / the pedagogy of the oppressed How does this one-with-the-people thing work exactly And / how do you actually / teach / people to read Paolo What skills do you teach and / how do you love as / an oppressor with / skills to impart The fear of saying / You / Must / Do / This / Because I Know More Than You / Because I Have Lived Longer / And Read More And Written More / stops my student teacher from choosing a path The path / is / in the students / she feels And of course / the path is in the students / but they are young / they are ignorant / they are waiting to be / taught

DISPATCH
in: the Hallway

AP Lit afterschool is   moments from starting I /   have barely
slammed a lesson together   Mrs. Carroll is not here yet   /   but her
students are and I do / not know them very well I do not know if I
have enough photocopies of these /   discussion prompts   or if they
are /   enough to fill the time   Q. and D. arrive   and D. asks / to
talk to me I suggest we talk in the hallway And this is my /   fuck
up   my mistake that can never be remedied   Q. objects I insist
and we stand in the hallway as D. tells me /   she is pregnant she is
due in   December   She cries and covers her / face with her hands
I well up but hide it by biting the inside of my   bottom lip I do /
my best to tell her that   yes she can still take AP Lit next year and
yes /   she can still graduate on time and yes I will do everything
I can   /   to make sure she gets there   And we're standing /   in
the hallway   Barely five minutes after the last bell   Students are
everywhere   There is nowhere /   more private nowhere I can take
her Nowhere that makes this /   better I am not /   up to this task
Q. has his arm around her I hug her too / all three of them / really
But it's more flailing than   hugging   more a way to hide my face /
obscure /   my lack of words   than   a gesture of comfort

DISPATCH
re: Faking It

I left the room to say hi to Mr. Barnes   and drop a student off at his class / then pee   When I came / back my student teacher was wiping tears from her face / again /   Her university advisor was telling her / all / the things I've told her   How many times does it take / till you learn it by watching   by doing   by failing   She can't / learn because I never really taught her   Not how I teach students / how / to interrogate a text / to write a complex thesis   to organize / a calendar of assignments   No one taught me / how to do this / either   I think / now / it is possible that the teacher who knows how to / teach / is exceedingly rare   I perform / my job as if on a stage   / and that I am good at   You should see / me dance   to a student drumming a pencil on the table   I perform / caring   too   Repeating / I like you   like having you in class   / I believe in you / You can do this   Even when the kid is near Shakespearean in his / villainy   when I know he / cheated on his homeless girlfriend and the homeless girlfriend will most certainly fail / as she hasn't done much all year / and who's gonna start trying in May of their senior year /   This year   though   I fake it much less   My student teacher will have to fake   everything for years   I tell her this   but what is it to teach   faking /   We all fake things   all the fucking / time   and students know / or they don't   because no one taught them how   the many ways faking it / are / real   love

DISPATCH
re: Big Dick

I am fuzzy with rye and heating pad   Yesterday Ms. Jay / walked into a chair or a desk and she swore in pain / Shit / Dick / Fuck And / just / so many dick jokes to be made   But I went with / You know I could really use some / dick   right about now When I bought / another bottle of rye at the state store tonight I thought of Claire / who I worked with at Tara Mandala She was / broke and we went to Whole Foods / She bought a giant bar of Kiss My Face / Big soap for the money / she said holding up the bar / to her face I grab the big bottle of Bulleit from the shelf / Big rye for the money Our / welcome back speech from the CEO last August was a / long long   speech about baseball and / I couldn't listen anymore because idgaf about baseball / but it ended with / 17 inches / 17 inches is our motto this year Apparently / that's the size of home plate and something something / we / don't change the size of home plate   whatever It was a bad / analogy and I couldn't follow beyond / the eight-minute anecdote about a ball player from decades ago But / boy howdy how many times did she say / 17 inches 17 inches / We at Frontier are committed to 17 / inches / It's hard but we persevere A long hard year / A nice big dick for the money

DISPATCH
re: the Blossom of Youth

If we had wanted to we could / have   toured the after-prom party at my high school   Saturday night   It was / open   to the public   Party like it's 1999   / My students were born   the year I graduated   My teenage years / are their party   decorations and / costumes   What is this generation's equivalent of   Ethan Hawke / wide-mouth kissing Winona Ryder   We / watched Ethan Hawke as Hamlet / in AP Lit and all guffawed   / But yinz / you   are missing the brilliance / of moody gen x Hawke   playing moody   / Hamlet   The white man   / with feels / shall inherit the earth   And they didn't understand   that Ethan Hawke was perfect / and garbage   all rolled into one   That's the / point   Now / could   we drink   hot blood   Monday and   all I want to do is   weep watching YouTube videos of / people singing in unison   / I watched the cast of *The Color Purple*   sing "Purple Rain" while I ate a strawberry popsicle on my prep   Only / two days until the AP Lit exam   / and / their / success hinges on whether they can / capture complexity   in their essays   / like how my childhood apple blossoms bloomed weeks ago   and I had no time   / to stand there and inhale   their perfume

YEAR THREE

DISPATCH
re: Our Scholars

> *Our society and its educational institutions seem to have*
> *lost sight of the basic purposes of schooling, and of the high*
> *expectations and disciplined effort needed to attain them.*
> —A Nation at Risk

Frontier is rewriting all / formal communications all website copy
/ slowly but not so subtly / to refer to students as scholars When
calling scholars' families / one policy begins Student centered
assessment practices are now / scholar centered assessment practices
What is the purpose of school I ask the students on the second /
day of the school year launching a weeks-long inquiry into / the
stated purposes and / implicit ends of American schooling In the
gallery walk a boy in a black and white photo sits facing the corner
/ dunce cap pointed at the ceiling / a series of graphs about family
income race and / SAT scores a TV still of Bart Simpson
writing / We do need no education line after line / on the
blackboard like a spell / or a curse *A Nation at Risk* suggesting
school undergirds American prosperity security civility / and
our schools' failures are due to a rising tide of mediocrity Civility
sticks / in my throat like a pill swallowed dry Schooling's
purpose / then is to encourage civility To be schooled is to / be
made courteous compliant Schooling's purpose / forever bound
by control And control a tool to create security and prosperity
/ but for whom Whom does it benefit asks Marx / though we
haven't studied Marxist theory / yet Whom does it benefit to call
students / scholars To take children of color and performatively
/ age them into such serious / stuffy academics Lock them away
in / an ivory tower until they / emerge civil and / obedient fit
to meet the nation's needs

DISPATCH

re: Colin Kaepernick

In thirty minutes of / enrichment / today I learned   my colleague
has successfully indoctrinated the students with propaganda I am
aware I am / not   unbiased My students are / most / definitely
aware   / are my students aware   /   But I had / no idea   how
quickly an honors   student with a facility for language / could take
a   dumbass thing said to her hours / before integrate it and state
it with the calm / certainty of fact   So /   do   / my students know
to disagree with my   points of view Have they ever been taught /
to disagree to marshal facts / logic   More horrifying / or less
/ that the teacher taught her students   that the American flag and
the Star Spangled Banner stand   for the military   and nothing /
else How could / that ever be true / Where is the line   between
deprogramming   and demanding allegiance / My patriotism is
/ true and would happily / kneel before the flag   /   My patriotism
is   / shameful and how can / you be shocked / anymore   that
this country isn't   / what it says it is I do / know   how easily
students will believe they   can   / pull themselves up by their own
bootstraps / that the path to riches is open / to all / that America is
the beautiful   the land of the   free / and they believe these things
innocently / while they casually mention their / first / friend who
/ was killed   While they call / out   offensive peers joking about
getting shot / Because that isn't funny when   you   had to leave
school for over a year / because you / were / shot While / they sit
in classrooms   / built by a system   / designed   on purpose / to
keep them / in their place /   where they can kneel / forever / for all
this country cares

DISPATCH
re: Potluck Love

Last year in AP Lit I / showed students a picture of myself pregnant
I had a red dress   enormous belly and /   a half-shaved head like the
punk /   I dreamed I was   Whoa Ms. B. with /   so much hair   said
a student   graciously not commenting on how big   nine-months
pregnant really /   is How inescapable the body /   when pregnant
D. is only seven months   but /   there is no missing that she /   is
pregnant   We circle up for advisory   and I have /   brought with
me a deck of cards /   each with a different emotion on its face and
three synonyms The /   game /   is called Tea & Empathy I need this
/ game I don't know /   what I'm doing   I ask students to choose
cards   one for /   how   they think   D. feels and /   one for how they
think   D.   wants to feel   For the first time /   this year   we have
an open conversation about how she is pregnant /   how they think
she might feel scared   excited   / anxious think she   wants to feel
loved   hopeful   supported   D. chooses cards herself for how she
feels and how she wants to feel   /   shows everyone how she feels
accepted in this /   small circle   We plan /   her baby shower   E.
writes everyone's name /   on a piece of poster paper and the kids /
volunteer to bring in decorations   pizza money /   buffalo chicken
dip those /   soft-baked cookies with the too sweet frosting For my
/   tiny advisory there is no /   love   like potluck love   where excess
is /   universal and paper plates sag with /   more cheese   more chips
more more /   more A half hour / when everyone's stomach strains
/   with joy   bliss   communion

DISPATCH
re: Pink

There is a beautiful velvet pink chair in the Arhaus / catalogue I
want that chair / in a sunny corner / which is to say I want / $1,299
and my house to face   the opposite direction / I want a chair / that
is mine   that faces the   morning sun and my face open / bathed
in the morning sun / Next to it / I will keep a large pile of / my
/ books and   / this tiny marble table   / $299 on sale   / holds my
hot tea   When I sit here / I think   / And when I curl up into it
/ my hips do not hurt and I don't have to worry / that I sit criss-
cross applesauce / all the time because my body / still works My
massage therapist   works on my face with her fingers / every other
week because there is a / single point   behind my nose / toward
which all of the muscles in my face draw in / and I cannot open
my face I only close it / tighter Yesterday she / worked her fingers
into the hard pink gums behind my / molars to release what I have
locked up / tight In my dream last night the pink was pepto pink
/ and I was going to a wedding with Mr. Barnes and Mr. Murray /
Murray had a pink tie / and Barnes wore pink trousers / and my
dress was the same pink pink pink / We were friends / We were on
a date / I felt / so loved / and supported In the dream / also then
a rabbit / fell from a water-rotted hole in the ceiling / into the high
school woodshop   / But I was   pinked / loved

DISPATCH
re: the Bud

> *The bud*
> *stands for all things,*
> *even for those things that don't flower,*
> *for everything flowers, from within, of self-blessing*
> —Galway Kinnell

Today   when R.   said / Not to come at your neck but / could you
not email / my mom when we have work / due I said it right back /
Not to come at / your / neck but / that sounds like a / you / problem
In the first Socratic seminar of the year R. argued the wage gap is a
myth   and entry-level computer programmers / should / make four
to five times as much / as seasoned early childhood educators / He
said that wasn't a gender   / thing at all   He sees less value   in the
bud   / than the blossom But / but but   I scream internally /
the bud stands / for all things / And this   is / you know /   a
gender thing   how he doesn't like   / women telling him what to
do even when one happens   to / know more than his 17-year-old
/ ass He definitely showed us / his whole ass back in September /
R. commandeered that seminar   to argue feminism / is outdated
when the seminar was about / the symbolic meanings of fire   and
he   was   / unprepared I finally got the class quiet today / and
writing   when someone sneezed and they all said / bless you bless
/ you   bless you / bless / you   until I cut in and / in my biggest
teacher voice / with support from the diaphragm / boomed I'll
give / you / a blessing How is that even a threat / the patriarchal
student asked But this / is my   worth   /   I will retell him in
words / and with love   how he holds inside   all things   until he
flowers /   from within   / of self-blessing

DISPATCH
re: White Out

This Wednesday we wore   white / to protest the black shirts the central office / requires us to wear   80-10-8   stamped across their fronts   / like we ever even knew what that meant   / Some goal something   blah blah   test scores   and it rhymes with / Good to Great / We are   great   to garbage fire this year / though   / and I feel like a ghost   white lace dress   white lace tights   / white cardigan white Fluevogs I am always /   more   than they expect   I look / around at my ghostly colleagues / and I fear   I was offered a crown because today I   am   the / ice queen In the Instruction and Culture Cabinet meeting   I once again   / melted   / when Principal Nash asked us to be a team   to / buy in I buy in   / I always / buy in Don't you / know I am on / your / side   And still I have to double check / at the meeting's end   that I was not   too / much   Too much is anything more   / than a yes-man   The traffic too / is too much   it takes me   an hour to drive home / When I arrive   I don't talk to my / family like I've been   looking forward   / to   Instead / I write about the day   / about the exhaustion   / about the students we do not serve   / I sublimate   / rage and become   this / ghostly   mist

DISPATCH
re: If/Then

Your task is to   write a   poem   that is composed entirely of if/
then statements   using the nouns   you draw /   from the hat   Use
juxtaposition / flagrantly   to find   connections / and resonances
among your   images and / thoughts

If I put   cotton   in the / hat then   the students   will write about
sacks and cotton / gins   If the apple trees bloom their pink / cotton
perfume   and the driveway / floods with   nostalgia   then / I'm
not sure I can   come back here tomorrow / and tomorrow   and
/ tomorrow If the lemon is a prop   then we pucker our mouths
sipping on /   lemonade   If the lemon is a character   / she walks
through the smoke   until her feet bleed and her   rind puckers If the
fresh asphalt   moans beneath / my wheels in the blueblack morning
then the forsythia   /   tangle and bloom in rashes along   the berm
If this school is a system / of interconnected   lies then I am an iron
fist in a velvet / glove   then I am an   iron system   / in a velvet lie If
routine is a banked   fire   Then I burn and burn and burn   like   an
/ unattended stove   If a teacher speaks of beauty   in / a crowded
room   then no / one hears her   when she falls

DISPATCH
re: the Circle of Power and Respect

At morning meeting   / standing in the circle of / power and respect
/ Mr. Barnes told us he was not coming / back next year   I can't /
explain how this   cleaves the building / collapses   the center   / of
the circle Except to say / two years ago / on a day of / reflection /
with a rowdy / disrespectful class of   / freshman I yelled / loudly
/ at kids / I did not know   to tell them / what a remarkable man /
stood in front of them / rooting for them   teaching them / loving
them And they / disregarded his presence   at their own / peril /
I / would never be as kind / as Barnes I warned   / I will / never
/ be as good as Barnes / And   now we've   used   him   up   I've
come to understand that   this is the job / too At the beginning
of every year / there is no time / to breathe and the body / will give
up   pushing to get / through / In the middle of the year / I will
learn how to / really / teach   this class / this book / this routine
/ this central question / But the   end   of the year will be always
an ending / How many people will not come back   How many
will / leave   because they cannot   push through   and that short
reprieve in the   middle   is not enough /   Can I keep doing this
/ waiting for   the beloved to leave / waiting for   a new   beloved
to emerge wobbling through a center / that will not hold

DISPATCH
from: the Bathroom

This is where I / cry   Another student lost   lost because we cannot / I cannot help enough Slam door slam door Slam and three doors between me / and the student I love / lost Toilet paper makes lousy / tissue and I / push my eyes deep / into my skull / I see /   stars receding into the black /   I am sure / people can hear me howling / down the hallway I can do / no more and now L.   is yelling at me / because I do not have enough handouts   I am empty handed when my hands should be / overflowing I am / overflowing and she cannot feel / my love / I love you but today others / have taken all the love I am found / wanting And I do / want a quiet warm space a happy ending / an ending at all

DISPATCH
re: Safety on the Boulevard

> *Then practice losing farther, losing faster:*
> *places, and names, and where it was you meant*
> *to travel. None of these will bring disaster.*
> —Elizabeth Bishop

At morning meeting   Principal Abbott   told us one of our students was shot / part of this ongoing   war / last night   The bullet went through his throat and out his cheek / but missed   killing   him / Abbott   had driven him to the   bus stop after school / because he didn't think it was / safe / to let him   / hobble on his crutches / all the way down the boulevard / to the bus stop   We / never / say die at   my school   / but this week   / I died / inside   a little more I told my AP kids / I was canceling / our extracurricular time   because I just / can't / keep / up   with the load   Tomorrow I will / quit   / again /   this time   from a committee   I should love   but   I   / am losing farther   / losing   faster / my hold on this /   life   I asked Ms. Long   Why does / this year feel like one   / long goodbye / How long do I   have left   to figure out how to   leave / you   / and these people   I /   love   These students   who are   so beautiful / there is no way to write   it / How to write   it   when this loss / will / bring disaster

LOVE LETTER
re: Red Shift

Dear student   Everything we do is for you / Dear student   you are / so dear   Dear student   May you never / see how much we do for you You are   weightless   / a spark of light   We are pitch / dark sky you are / brilliance   Dear student You are moving so fast / so far / my eyes see only / red Dear student If only you / knew   how much we / would do / for you   Dear student We love you   We / love I love I love you I / love you   I   love

I love

    I love

      you

DISPATCH
re: More

What I want is a long bath with *Downton Abbey* fizzy water / and
my face slathered in thick white clay I want / more Manhattan
another expensive cherry maybe just another glass of rye   nothing
/ else required   No / I want the cherry   I want the cherry on top
of / this week I want   more times when my students pretend /
to be Spider-Man   and throw themselves sideways at the lockers
outside the classroom   door and fewer times when my yelling at
/   underclassman is interrupted by a student   vomiting under my
desk into a trashcan More   potlucks and fewer echoes of how Mrs.
Berry's voice broke / talking about L. who was murdered / a week
ago the wild / wailing of her sobs   The New York City Department
of Education mailed me   /   more money this week   It's been five
years / since I left and still /   the arrears   appear in the mailbox
This year /   it was less than $10 and I am mad that this /   blood
money / We always call it blood / money   when it follows me
here / This blood money will cost me   more / in paperwork and tax
preparation fees than / the dollars in the   check What   luxuries
have I bought with my / blood money   Cherries blood red   Day
long / hangovers   indolent and / wan Thick white clay from the
/ potter's field to smear across my / face   like   so much whiteness

DISPATCH
re: We mustn't dwell, no not today

Bless   Netflix for *Empire Records*   / even tho I already have it on
Blu-ray   / My friend   Joanna   from college   watched it and said
/ I don't get it   Flippantly / I told her it was too   late for her   But
then   / I meditated on / why it's such   a soft   blanket   a cozy fire of
dancing flames   /   It's like how Mr. Murray bought Ms. Long   /
a SpongeBob popsicle from the Family / Dollar on Friday because
he knew she loved them   / and there they were   in their   cotton
candy flavored   glory   / at the checkout as he waited   to pay for
his chips   Like how the / joy   spread   across her face as she picked
SpongeBob's bubblegum eyes off in the staff lounge / to save for
later   That / is *Empire Record*s   /   the tattooed gum chewing freaks
love   / even as they fight   / and their beloved record store   succumbs
to amoral corporatization   Yes   they / do / think they're so happy
and so / goddamn great   / because they   draw together   like a /
family hunkered in a basement   waiting   / for a storm to pass   We
are waiting out   / this / storm   We are laughing in the staff lounge
at how Murray saw a bird   eating a chicken wing   in the parking
lot   and /   even my colleagues who do not look for / metaphors
in everything understand   / the grimness of / this / one   Are we
drawing together for support   or   are we eating each other   to sate
our   / personal hungers   We laugh   again   We do not / question   for
we mustn't dwell   no / not today   When the credits roll   and one
day / they will   we know we   will / dance on the rooftop   with
hands joined

DISPATCH

re: Summer Lee's Speech at Graduation

This year's graduation speaker almost didn't get to speak / Summer
Lee who just won a landmark / landslide upset in a state house
race / over a machined and moneyed incumbent She / ran on an
anti-charter school platform / and our CEO was / nervous / our /
CEO / does not trust a politician who knows how to / school the
public / But Summer Lee grew up in the same neighborhoods /
as my students and she told them / I know how hard you / had
to work to get here And / I know / if you look around / you will
remember / your friends / who didn't make it here / Then I cry just
for a moment / E. is here now in the audience / She was Glinda
the Good in last year's school production of *The Wiz*   I cried then
too   to watch her on stage / So loud so capacious a   performer
literally /   a scene stealer   in piles of petticoats and   a comical
top hat   In March   because it wasn't enough to kick / her out of
school she / also   got kicked out of / the musical's opening
night because she / reeked of weed /   There was no /   almost
for / her   just / no   thank you I love her for coming   here
to cheer   for her friends / in   their decorated mortar boards   and
fancy shoes I grieve for her /   in her ball cap and crocs watching /
from a distance   as others receive what she / too worked so hard for

DISPATCH
re: the Last Day of School

The seniors / have graduated and the tenth graders / have finished
their portfolios   Only ninth and eleventh graders remain but even
they / are gone because the grades   are submitted   the year is
done / and only those with the strictest of parents / remain   Also Q.
my favorite senior   who walked across the stage   his parents /
beaming in the audience   / is still here   First to graduate   in his
family   only he hasn't / actually / graduated   His senior project
remains undone   We hound him   / around the building   There's
some kind of problem with / his phone   not being charged   so he
can't finish / this video   Why do I not hound him   / harder   sit on
him /   for real   / in my room   where I can keep an eye on him
Hours later   / the final bell rings   and we are in Mr. Murray's room
trying / to make Q.'s new iPhone talk to the old iMacs   but it is
useless   He   / half asses something and I text Ms. Jay   / so she
can see it and he can officially / graduate   She is gone   already   and
I have a text from Ms. Sullivan   asking if I am still in the building
Yes / I am still here   what do I tell Q.   tell Jay to / fucking / text
me back   Can you bring the cakes   she asks   I forgot them   So I am
carrying   two giant layer cakes for Mr. Abbott's retirement / party
already underway   and I tell Q.   he failed / again / Ms. Rupert
who was my student teacher / is leaving   too   for good   and she
won't be back   for the end of year / party   So I say good/bye to
her   for maybe   forever   I cry / in the car   in the parking lot of /
Peppers N'AT   and look forward to a drink with my colleagues   /
who will understand   Inside they are already / tipsy   and past the
point of / processing   So   why am / I / here   Who   here   / can
help   me

YEAR FOUR

DISPATCH
re: Stabbing Potatoes

At lunch we watched a video about how to / stab a raw   potato
with a straw   / You aim / past the potato and shout / follow
THROUGH as you stab / I wonder / often / if this is real life /
I wonder   / what would happen if I didn't come back / didn't teach
/ the freshmen in my advisory who won't listen / how to stab   / a
potato / clean through with a straw   Another day / at lunch / we
all laughed   about how we'd each imagined / on the road   in the
early morning / the asshole speeding down the highway   / and we
wondered / You know if I got in a car wreck / at least I could / lie
down for a bit / in the quiet   What would / giving up look like   /
A teacher with a potato   in her hand / surrounded by a classroom
of / 14-year-old   / strangers who have forgotten she exists

DISPATCH
re: the Moon

On mornings like this one   I try and / fail   to capture the moon
I know   too clever by half   /   but it's true   It hovers just above
the Giant Eagle   a white eye like the / vulture's   bright but hiding
behind   a nictitating membrane Pocked   bewitching   And the
photo is nothing   never more than / the distant moon always less
than   the obsession Brett Kavanaugh's face is at / the top of all
the websites   Pale   white   only a hint of red   /   on his snarl   In
class   I project   pictures of / Anita Hill   and Clarence Thomas
alongside Kavanaugh We / compare and contrast   and the kids are /
horrified by this man these men   I imagine Kavanaugh's spittle /
splattering the stand   It would be a joke if it weren't   so /   painful
C. asks if he will be confirmed and I /   tell her   Yes   /   he will
There's some small chance /   still but it's clear   his performance will
/   succeed   Behind the mask of rage   another mask   of certainty
Or maybe there is no   mask and male rage   is inseparable from
power / I tell C.   later that she was / in   my dream   We were in my
classroom and I was /   holding her hand   pulling / her along behind
me as we ran out and down the hallways   Why / she asked and I
said   O. / a freshman in Creative Writing /   was being attacked by
someone   a / bad man / beyond the parking lot   in the flowering
bushes behind Giant Eagle   that smell like /   summer   We ran
through   the front /   doors   across the parking lot   Abruptly   I
stopped   and turned back   Where are you going   dream C. asked
/ dream me   The withholding moon again / above us   beneath
our feet   shimmering in the dew-kissed asphalt   Inside /   I said
shrugging   /   It's too late

DISPATCH
re: Biblical Plagues

In the bathroom   I flushed the toilet and it backed up   / the water
turned   to / blood   The Toad   / sits heavy in my chest   Another /
toad   squats so hard upon   Ms. Katz that she will quit   / tomorrow
/ to be rid of it   The toads   / squat on us all   The rain   / fell in
sheets and we were / cast into darkness   during 5th period   / lunch
The terror   of being a freshman / in a blackened restroom   /   Last
week   / another bedbug   /   No one informed   us but we knew   it
was   / in the back hallway   / where the previous plague of   bedbugs
flourished   and closed the school /   for days   / Yet another colleague
/ crushed by the plague of the toad   / left our school   / to find   her
new classroom   / swarming with snakes   / Or you know   / just
one creepy snake skin the old teacher left behind   / The   swarms
of snakes   / are   / actually /   at one of our network's   elementary
schools   / Tomorrow   is a potluck   an   / obvious analogue   for
a plague of locusts   / starving for   whatever we can   get

DISPATCH
re: Gag

At the end / of my sophomore year of college I had a lump in
my throat for / weeks   I gagged on almost all   food   I / was
generally a miserable   / girl far from home   and / living in an
unairconditioned / Baltimore   rowhouse in June / Sitting in the
Borders / I read about blocked throat chakras and then I went to
eat some Chik-fil-A / because chicken nuggets went down   / fine
What truth   / was   I swallowing   then My husband says I have
always been filled with   righteous / indignation   But I swear / I
never used to be   so angry   / so angry all the time all the time all
the time   / I cannot feel / sadness anymore / When Katz told us
she was quitting / I   felt   / nothing / then relief / some form of
happiness / for her / and resignation   A minute later and I / just
/ went about my day / on fire   My new ninth graders / act like I
am   nothing a / nonhuman / below   regard / So I do yoga /
to open my throat and unblock   / the smoky hum   / of expression
/ I seek my blue sky body What / bullshit I can barely even write
it / But at least   I can check / yoga off the list   so there's that I /
am noisy mind / mute throat and burning / energy flaming from
my root   / up through the column of my body Flames / devour
my truth   I / seek that truth and find   / ash   in my throat   I gag
I / swallow still

DISPATCH
re: this Darkness

A dark scrim obscures this year / from me My room is dark / the
skylight admits / gray   light   rain   light and the students are /
kept from me The new gradebook software is / impenetrable and
hidden from the students / We do not know   how to / evaluate
their work and they   / cannot see the data   when we do   Notice
how I called feedback / data   The students talk so much / I am
obscure / and obscured / fading in plain sight I cannot / penetrate
and I cannot see My advisory is bad   my advisory is the worst
group of students I have /   ever   / taught   failed   to teach   I
cannot be / real My whole schtick is being / real   But when I am
real   they / laugh   They asked / Ms. Beddow   were you ever /
bullied and I / paused because no but also / does a year of slut-
shaming count / as bullying It must it hurt / so much   but I do
not know   In that pause   / they laughed   and I left / the room to
stand in the hallway because / how do I stand in a room   with more
kids who will / litigate my adolescent traumas   and find them /
insignificant I cannot   write this anymore I write and the poem
remains / dark and impenetrable Do these connections / connect
Is there anything of meaning   here

DISPATCH

re: How to Run a Restaurant

There was this one time when a waitress   at a fancy restaurant /
misfired my dinner order and our whole wine plan was / dashed
My date was a sommelier in training   Goddamn life was different
/ in my twenties The problem   / as he diagnosed it / was not   a
dumb mistake made by a server   but that the server was unable / to
go to her sous chef to fire a new dish   or her manager to comp some
dessert   The culture / was toxic so the service was both expensive
/ and /   poor The education / at Frontier is / expensive and /
poor / A rotating cast of / baby teachers   continually replacing
the previous year's babies   who / quit at the rate of 20% per year
wastes / more than   real money   We are in the middle of / another
failed initiative This / standards-based grading pilot   was a good
/ idea to improve instruction / achievement /   outcomes /
our image   with the Department of Education   Now it is / another
predictable   failure   driving   three principals   and dozens of
teachers to   / save themselves   skip the hassle   to /   quit the
summer before it began   What stopped   Osborne from   / talking
to the CEO   to others at the central office   / Why did he not /
delay the rollout   ensure / it was   done right from the   start
When he listens to us   he only hears   his / beautiful ideas
repeated / back to him like we're waitresses repeating his order
to serve him /   well   He sees scallop quenelles / delicate and
preciously plated   served / with a hearty red wine   What riches
we serve here   he thinks / to himself

DISPATCH

re: A Discipline Action Has Been Assigned To [name redacted]

Mr. [Redacted]   I did not hear from you yesterday [when you forgot to call me]   I believe action needs to be taken   to address the conflict between Ms. Beddow   and [name redacted]   [my daughter who cursed out Ms. Beddow to her face]   [my daughter who was   willfully out of dress code two days in a row] [my daughter who was warned politely and playfully the first day and still decided not to follow rules] [my daughter who called   Ms. Beddow a stupid bitch   in front of a room of students] I   believe in discipline and not   punishment

I am concerned [name redacted] reported to two teachers   [what teachers though] that   Ms. Beddow   allegedly threw binders [they were student planners] [the goddamn giant planners that no one uses because they are unusable and are not three-hole-punched either] to the floor and locked students in the room [for five minutes so they could finish the lesson   because they wasted well more than five minutes] [for five minutes   while another teacher and the assistant principal were there] Per [name redacted] Ms. Beddow has no control over her students   her students talk back to her [This is true   it is my shame] [my skin burns   my heart flares into my throat] [There is no explanation] [i cannot explain what it feels like to be stripped of power and respect and efficacy] [it is too much to bear] [what it is like to be treated as invisible] [my invisibility   hides   this shame] [i understand i have all the privileges and all the institutional power] [But also   do i have all the power   if i hide in the bathroom after class] It appears you did not investigate the allegations [Of course he talked to me about it i cried in his office] [Or i just cried in the staff lounge i cry too often

to remember all the wheres] How do I file a complaint   If I do
not hear from you I will be filling a report with Childline [She will
file a report with Childline] [She will file a report with Childline]
[i am abusive i shouldn't have thrown   those student planners]
[i yell   too much] [i will lose my career] [She will file a report
with Childline] [i won't even be allowed to volunteer   at my kids'
school] [after i lose my job] [after i lose my career] [She will file
a report with Childline] If you have any concerns please feel free to
reach out to me   Thank you.

DISPATCH
re: Childline

I suppose   I   / should / be grateful this woman   this mother didn't report   / me to Childline I have lost / faith in who I am / here / I am / ineffective   /   my words   fall like ash   / on the proceedings / weighing nothing and noticed little / except as annoyance   / Another volcanic   explosion   / from Beddow   /   Pay no mind she'll / blow over soon enough I am / data in the   spreadsheet and / lost For one   / I am   racist   / For two / I am abusive   /   The writers in my writing class   / are all failing   /   save three   These numbers   / are incantations   /   I always knew I would have to leave / when the math failed   When what I got   / was less than the price   / extracted   The 8 panicked texts / I sent   received only / 1 answer   from a text group of 7   There's a magic / in this text chain   / If someone responds by 8pm / I will stay   If I have messages / in the morning by 5am / I will stay   I will stay   / I can't stay Divination by text message / No responses yet Yet this magic is more powerful than I / realized

DISPATCH
re: Usage Error

I had an idea   earlier   But ideas   barely live here /   anymore I
yelled / at Osborne   now the senior director of schools grades 6-12
/ after I shared with him / what I thought / was a fine example
of student writing   and the first thing he said was / Look   she's
missing a comma after the introductory phrase The second / thing
he said was / Also   you don't start a paragraph with /   on the
one hand / He then played a game of / keep away with the paper
/ over the staff lounge table / and that   was the end of me The
second / end of me because I had already spent / a period crying
in my car / texting in the cold / unable to face the inside of the
/ school again / uncertain how to stay in a / building where I feel
physically unsafe / emotionally / busted Yesterday a student picked
up / a   tub of cocoa butter and feigned as / to throw it and I /
flinched   Another student   / in the dead quiet of eighth period
when no students are in the senior hallway / slammed his body /
against the wall   and the whole wall shook He slammed his body
against my wall   / and I almost burst into tears Last night / my
husband slammed a melamine plate / on the table because our son
wouldn't / eat his dinner and I almost / burst into tears   I could try
/ now / to braid together these images / of slamming of / flinching
of keep away / of the lost ideas and the fingers   too cold / to text
But I can / not   because I sense an error in this / parallelism There
is no diagram for   such / battered syntax

DISPATCH
re: the Interior

I want   nothing so much as   / access to the interior   I crave   /
inward   gaze of secrets and intimacy with   / myself   All I am
today is   hard   / salt crusted and calcified a tessellated carapace
Nothing / connects   My students expect   / me to control them
serve as an external / restraint stopping   them from / breaking rules
such as Do not leave the room during class   and Do not swear   all
the   time   /   H. was furious with me /   offended   when I told
her she had the inner / resources to control herself F. tattles all the
time Ms. Beddow / he won't put me down   make him put   / me
down G. always asks me to   / write someone up when that someone
/ annoys her But   I cannot control a dozen   students   like they
are   / avatars and I am / the only   / autonomous   / person here
twiddling a joystick and choosing weapons from / a menu If / they
expect me to   stop their mouths with   dirty socks and duct tape   /
bind their limbs with   / zip ties force their / knees to buckle and
/ buckle them to the chairs   This / is not who I am   I have lost /
myself   to my /smallest mistakes which they repeat / to me over
and over / while laughing I stifle / my shame my / larger mistakes
which I cannot look at directly   and tell myself I am / only denying
these bullies   a reaction / These bullies are   /   children I am a
spinning lodestone finding no / course through   the innermost
country There is no path   through / the pitch that sticks   the
darkness   the whatever it is / within

DISPATCH

re: my Feminine Wiles

> *stealin my shit from me/ dont make it yrs/ makes it stolen/*
> *somebody almost run off wit alla my stuff/ & i waz standin*
> *there/ lookin at myself/ the whole time*
>
> —Ntozake Shange

Osborne managed to / again / blow off my concerns about this
standards-based grading pilot / by cunningly emailing a / pseudo
/ apology for that time a week ago when he / insulted my teaching
and / laughed like / Ha ha aren't we just / joking I have not
felt / my gender / so clearly in ages When I was in high school I
went to / Mr. Romano my high school band teacher to say / I was
learning saxophone so could I join / the jazz band When I talked
to him / he was on the rostrum looking down on me He said /
That's really sweet of you to be / learning   But you're really going to
have / to buckle down and master the / notes / I was in all the
/ honors bands I was a section leader in the marching / band Mr.
Romano rarely / remembered my name called me / Caitlin a lot /
But he did once yell at the band's president for not being more
like / me   When my current administrators asked the Instruction
and Culture Cabinet members / of which I am one / to weigh in on
fixing our crushing staff morale problem / I invested / a full prep
period   to an email diagnosing our loss of credibility as a staff and
suggesting / we focus on rebuilding that credibility / focusing
our efforts on student motivation / one element of which is /
yes / teacher credibility Becker the instructional coach / today
/ gave a PD on student motivation / citing the very materials I
recommended   / said he would be teaching a full day of it   / in
January / I listened to my ideas come out of his mouth my own

mouth / muted / And it's like   I am not here   I am / divorced
from my   /   thoughts   I am told again and again to join   the /
team   buckle down   But I already know   / these notes   you fuckers
I   give them / to you and you / ignore them   I give   them to you
/ and you take them   / as your own   I'm / here   I'm   / here /   I'm
performing the whole / damn song

DISPATCH
re: All may be well

> *"Oh, speak of that. That do I long to hear."*
> —Claudius in *Hamlet*

In year four of teaching *Hamlet*   I find I only   /   hear Claudius echoing / in my thoughts   That / do I long to   hear   /   Or   more devastatingly   Bow   knees /   be soft as sinews   of the newborn   / babe   My offenses   are rank   /   too   Two years ago   Bette died / of cancer   in her early 70s   I have an essay about Bette   the owner of the   California diner   where I waited tables   in my twenties   / that is incomplete and only   really   about / me   When Bette was in my   life   /   she was more   beneficent presence   than   human /   The essay is a failure   and maybe this poem can   /   make up   its lack   Bette was the invisible and   /   ever present scent of / jasmine   wrapping me in   warmth /   in   a state   3000   miles from everyone   / I knew and loved   How do I write about her   / when I was   self-involved   and she   was   /   the air   I   never / wrote the letter   to the diner   and her / husband   who cared   for me / too   This year   my stepmom   is fighting her third round of cancer   /   This year   it may / be fatal   Tonight my kids told her / you look like a crazy evil   wizard   because she is bald   and they finally watched Harry Potter for the / first time   Where was   I   / rewriting habit targets and   /   thinking deeply about *Like Water for Chocolate*   and how I can link it   thematically   to the Troubles / Trouble   hardening   my heart to strings of / steel   I cried so much less   / this year   No more   for me / unmanly griefs   Rather a heart / fortified against   /   a mind   patient   with / death   that / common theme   Nothing left   / but   gestures   toward   all / may be well

DISPATCH
re: I'm so sorry

> *'now i know that you know i love ya, but i aint ever gonna love ya like want me to love ya, i'm sorry'*
> —Ntozake Shange

I   make it a point to refuse mentoring   / seniors on their senior projects I have too many / courses to teach   I say So sorry   But this year   Z.   is a senior and   her project is on sexism / in the literary world I could have /   said no But really even if I said no   Z. knows how to use Google comments   and how to tag   me in them / I have read her /   novel   in pieces   for / years now   And she would surely be / tagging me into her senior paper   multiple times a day by now whether I was her mentor / or not   So   after an expert I hooked her up with blew her off   I step in An expert   I tell her the story about / publishing an essay about someone else's abuser   using his / name blowing up the feminist poetry collective helping   / shut down the abuser's press   the abuser's legal threats   I am not / sorry   I would do it again   even as I   doubt   I will ever do something like that / again   I am /   from time to time   sorry   the collective is / gone   I am sorry I did not   give the collective's leader /   my idol   a heads up   that I was setting fire to / everything I'm sorry   she was a sorry leader who   didn't / anticipate her downfall   better I'm sorry she /   disappointed us all   I am sorry   I /   had an idol   to begin with   I am / sorry   all the time   now I am sorry my friend /   Z.'s expert /   blew her off   I am sorry for that time I tried to blow off my mom   and accidentally / smacked her in the face in front of my friends in   the movie theater lobby   I'm / sorry I threw the student planners   and now we all hate each other and / will never   dig our way out of our antipathies   I'm sorry I made D.   tell me / she was

pregnant in the hallway at dismissal I'm sorry / that I hate listening
to my voicemails and missed my friend's   surprise / wedding that
I could have / afforded to   attend   if only I wasn't a sorry teacher
sorry daughter sorry friend finding reasons to / be busy to   leave
the scene   I am sorry I leave early   to do committee / work at the
central offices and linger /   in my car before going inside   I am so
sorry   that even when I get home / I leave to some place inside /
myself away from my / children   I am so sorry I am so   so sorry
I will /   do it all   again

DISPATCH
re: Frank Romano

I'm sorry   I can't / let this go I have more / to say   about Frank Romano / and the patriarchy When I first told the story of how Romano / scoffed at me   when I asked to join the / jazz band / that same night at the dinner table with my family / my step/mom was outraged on my behalf but my / dad   said / I'm sure he didn't mean / it   like that   But I / I was / sure and my step/mom was sure The only girl in the jazz band played / piano   Would I have been more useful as / something other than a horn / player Imagine a girl   with / a horn   Is there a version of this story where that   old man /   retired when he should have or bothered /   to know me my name even   My point / though / the point is that even when I was / 17 I was taught / to doubt my perceptions told to leave the / subtext   buried and button down / my intuition   Now / is a year-long flickering of gaslights   We have meetings In them / I am on fire / with righteous   fury and intelligent solutions My colleagues agree nod their heads take / notes Then / the next day / nothing happens / everything happens again   I offer solutions for the greater good / not my own ego A man then takes them as his rightful / due   I am a tool an instrument / but the wrong one   Like that old scrap of shopping list in the passenger seat of the car you use like / floss to dislodge a piece of apple from between / your teeth Good enough in the moment and it gets the job done but / in the end / not even worth   a name

DISPATCH

re: Domain 4f Showing Professionalism

> *Accomplished teachers have a strong moral compass and are guided by what is in the best interest of students. Such educators display professionalism in a number of ways. For example, they conduct their interactions with colleagues with honesty and integrity. They know their students' needs and seek out resources in order to step in and provide help that may extend beyond the classroom. Teachers advocate for their students in ways that might challenge traditional views and the educational establishment, seeking greater flexibility in the ways school rules and policies are applied.*
> —Charlotte Danielson's *Framework for Teaching*

I stood   naked in my classroom / yesterday   At work at 6:45
in the morning and   graduation started at 6pm   so I could / not
go home   I papered over the door's window / changed into a
t-shirt   and played a yoga video on the SmartBoard   / I moved
rhythmically and with purpose to / settle   stress   Afterwards
I took it all / off   No need for anything /   but freshness   I was
/ new   and whole   Later that evening in no more than twenty /
minutes   I took selfies with / every graduating senior   I talked
to older brothers   older sisters   last year's graduates   This / is
what I cannot take with me   /   Next year   even more   siblings /
their faces smiling beneath blue / mortar boards   / will hang on
the wall   / of selfies above my desk Today   / I received my year/
end evaluation and   was   .05 points / short of the full merit
raise   I / remain invested in   metrics and praise   a portrait of
/ ambition   My principal docked me a point / on professionalism
What interactions   / have I had   marked by / dishonesty   I am
honest / to my own detriment When   / my moral compass   points
/ me down an unmarked path   I make of / myself a pain   a nag
a   grind in the / gears of the establishment Stripped / to nothing

I have looked inside / myself I replay / the times I have failed
my / students the times I've yelled slammed the door so hard /
dust fell from the molding the times the lesson was / bad or
my / curricular choices shortsighted But no amount of reflection
will reveal to me how to be / professional in a system so
broken it / shreds me leaves me a corpse in underwear and an
ancient / t-shirt spread / on the classroom floor

YEAR FIVE

DISPATCH
re: Advocacy

The push is on this   year / for the educators at Frontier Schools to take part in the /   charter network's lobbying efforts   Our CEO reminds us / regularly that   we are in an uncertain political climate and our /   students' rights are being trampled by a Governor   out to get /   us   There was some concern last year that the state would not renew the charter on one of our K-8s that / the ship may / this time   / sink But despite the 48%   proficiency rates   our students' / right to   this slightly less failing school was /   preserved For two years / anyway The engines run on   data   /   Scores for / everything   Our budgets our raises our students' / promotions to the next grade   Last year /   every employee in my school   lost out on   money because our   / Building Wide Score / a measure based on a rubric that Frontier never /   showed us / pulled down our personal eval scores What does go into that / score   Does it / accommodate for   how many teachers quit Does it /   reward the teachers who /   pick up   that discarded load / ha /   Teachers quit / all the time here The political waters are / dark and storm-tossed As it is above   so it is / below   A storyteller on the radio once talked about trying to get help /   for addiction or homelessness or both /   I can't remember   exactly /   But he described the help offered as a kit /   to build a boat   Not /   an actual boat   And that is / how it is   here   We are given the tools   the raw materials / endless spreadsheets   of data We are told   Build   build anew build tight and strong   based on these findings Make this ship   / yare And we try   We sit   we analyze the / data We make   new plans   All the while the sea rises   The sea washes   us / one by one   away

DISPATCH
re: In my bag

When I get dressed   in the morning / I dress for my   students
Specifically /   I dress for   four students   in my /   eighth period
English class   When I look particularly /   myself in the mornings
I think /   K. will tell me today that I am   in my bag   I am fully
in my bag /   Today   I wear my rose gold glitter   eight hole Doc
Martens /   new   but also   it is twenty years later and still I'm
wearing   Docs   I wear /   a chiffon   dress with an empire waist
and   lace   tights   Ms. Beddow   you are in /   your bag today   K.
says   nodding and appraising   Why thank /   you   I thought you /
would say that I say as I   strike a few poses   Picture me   Winona
Ryder   in *Reality Bites*   but older and   a touch teacherly   a bag full of
cheesy tricks   for / hooking students   slung over   my shoulder   We
sit /   elbow to elbow   at the center table   The students   write big /
beefy paragraphs and I   read Twitter   think idly about /   grading
Periodically   I remind them to actually   you know   write /   and
not just talk   talk   talk some more /   I join their conversation about
/   homecoming dresses /   My homecoming dress   was /   cut down
to a few inches above my   butt   and my mom /   freaked out   I say
Until I remember   to tell them /   again   Write!   I move back to my
desk /   for   more space   some air /   of my own   and then I scroll my
mind   dead   This day is /   almost   in the bag   I am /   a windbag
out of   wind   From the center table   in a /   small voice   K. says
Where'd you go   Can't you see I've packed /   my bags   I think I don't
want /   to come back   Baby /   K. says voice   small /   come back

DISPATCH
re: Shoutouts at the Morning Meeting

Shout out to   Beddow for showing up every day   Shout out to
Beddow for / reworking the advisory plans every week / because
freshmen still can't sit in a circle   Shout / out to Beddow / for
teaching   / three / different courses and fully / prepping each
one   / each week before she even leaves the building on Friday
/ afternoons Shout   out to Beddow for /   the complexity and
challenge in the Playing with Fire essays the AP Lit / kids have to
write Shout out to Beddow for / the website she built   filled with
supplemental materials on the history of Singapore and comics so
the kids will / understand *The Art of Charlie Chan Hock Chye* /
when they read it Shout / out to Beddow for warning us about all
that could go wrong   / with standards-based grading   Shout out /
to Beddow for explaining the same shit over / and over to kids and
grown-ups / alike Shout out to Beddow / who we do not listen to /
because she is always / fine   Shout out to Beddow / who predicted
all that is happening now   Shout shout shout shout / out to Beddow
who is so far away   / in the senior hallway she / can't hear us   Shout
out / to Beddow who is so far away   / she is going   going / gone

DISPATCH
re: Who jammed the photocopier?

Manners   hold that / if you jam the photocopier   then you / unjam
the photocopier   Or / at the very least / post a sad note and tell
Jasmine   the / administrative assistant   so she can put in a / repair
ticket   Naturally /   I spend a lot of time / here / unjamming   /
other people's messes   In the middle of fourth period   today   the
entire English team   / across all three high schools / received an
email informing us that the new curriculum   / which I wrote with
Jay and   Taylor   / was canceled and /   a new one for next   year
would be chosen by a new / curriculum team   Please apply   /
Osborne   and Leah   / I sat in their office last night   planning next
week's PD   and / they didn't say a word   / I read the email aloud /
to fourth period   Their mouths are agape   They didn't even   say it /
to our faces   Those assholes   I run down the hallway to Jay's room
and tell her to check her email   I hear / from my classroom door   B.
asking Ms. Long   /   Does that mean kids won't learn what we're
learning /   and K. saying   That's fucked up   During lunch   we sit
in the breakroom   I'm done crying now   Outrage and numbness
- an intoxicating cocktail / thrumming in my synapses   Long says
/ Leah   sorry to say it   she's like a white piece of paper   What's
even there /   The racial implications / are   text here   not subtext   I
say   No / Leah is the photocopier   mindlessly copying established
practices   and I'm the paper / jamming up the works   She's trying
/ to rip me out /   Kay laughs   She thinks / she unjammed you this
time   But poor / Leah   doesn't know how to fix anything   I say /
I know   But also /   I'm the paper jammed in the photocopier   I'm
/ that piece that got wrinkled up like a fan   a chunk / torn off and
now I'm pressed against the fuser   about /   to catch fire

DISPATCH
re: the Wick Dipper in the Anthropologie Candle Accessories Set

I   once read a woman's story about how / she became addicted to
a high / level of productivity   to the / adrenaline   rush of pressure
and tasks and accomplishment   When / she quit her demanding
job she had an awful / come down   but it was only then that she
realized   how hard how fast how un/livable her life had / been   I   am
never still / I am never / unoccupied   When my principal suggested
calling parents on my commute as a time-saving measure   I told
him / I already work in the car   / by listening to the audiobooks
of whatever I am   about / to teach I know how   to multitask I am
more than   / burning a candle at both ends   I am wicks on wicks
on wicks   eating wax like cotton candy /   I am working harder
than / ever because I am   distancing myself   from / my colleagues
from / the children   How do you fix   the problems   and leave the
problems   at / once   I learned about / wick dippers   as I browsed
the internet for candles while burning candles while watching *Grey's
Anatomy* while lesson planning   /   Instead of blowing out a candle /
smoking up the room   you use the wick dipper   to dip the flaming
wick   under the wax   and it is a / smokeless snuff   Here   now   /
how   do / I   snuff myself / without smoking

DISPATCH
to: Leah

Shake it up is all that we know
Using the bodies up as we go
—Hall & Oates, "Out of Touch"

Dear Leah   I wanted to send this quick email /   to let you know officially that   I did not apply again for the curriculum / development pathway But I also want to say   I fear you think   I don't like /   you   I like you /   fine   I remember sitting in Miller's packed up /   classroom   two summers ago   and we listened to   so much Hall & Oates unpacking standards and mapping learning targets   /   on countless posters and the dingy   whiteboard wall   It felt like we /   were building something   Even if that thing   refused / understanding   used up / everything we /   gave it and /   more   Because what did we know   about / how to write a curriculum   how to write a learning target framework how / even the new gradebook software would work How quickly the district /   would change it up on us   In my dreams last night   you were my husband and we were /   moving into a new   apartment   in New York City   but it /   was so big   A railroad apartment with   / a second railroad storage room   along the side   Old chairs and dust   like you would expect /   jumbled that storage room but the cubbies /   So many storage cubbies and all /   empty   waiting to be filled   In this dream   we had   two daughters   and they / were exploring the storage   rooms with me Beneath our feet the / gaps in the floorboards were just slightly   too big   and when / the girls bounced on their toes in excitement   the floorboards /   swayed and bowed   I told you /   reluctantly   I don't think we can build here I'm afraid / we will all   fall through

DISPATCH
re: Out of joint

The lady doth protest   too much   That was from *Hamlet* before it
was a cliché   Ditto the scam notion that / There is nothing either
good or / bad   but thinking / makes it so   I protested / vociferously
my lack of burnout   Insisted to my husband / I am doing   so well
I barely work / at home   / at   all anymore   I have mastered   / my
content   the course progression   the texts   Look   / I can even
quote *Hamlet*   at length   / and /   enjoy it   I pushed so hard before
/   but now   /   I have found the /   balance   A few years ago   /
around this time   I had an endless   /   case of pinkeye   The only
relief I could find / came from crying   Last year   /   my skin was
so dry and my lips so chapped   Nothing I did   /   helped   for
weeks   until   /   finally I smeared coconut oil and honey   over
everything for / days   This year   /   despite my thinking   I was
good   angular / cheilitis   endlessly for   / the past two   months   /
Red flakes   in the corners of my mouth   that clear up   come back
/ clear up   / come back   I read a book about burnout   /   A sign of
burnout   is infections   /   illnesses   that don't clear up   That's
the body's   protest   But aye there's the / rub   rubbing me   red and
/ raw   Turns out my body   will   /   not be denied   And I cannot
no matter   what I do /   protest   fight   its too too solid flesh   /
melting

DISPATCH
re: Another Universe

Eighth period and   W. is asleep /   again   He came in all smiles
Ms. B.   My favorite teacher / how are you   and now   ten minutes
later   no amount of knocking on his table will /   raise him   to
consciousness   I know he   stays up / too late playing video games
working on his / drawings   I know because he was featured in / the
local paper   in a story   about kids who   / the school system left
behind   He connects / with others   through headsets   Ever   since
L. / was killed   two years ago   was / shot   W.'s anxiety / turned
his neighborhood into / a malevolent place   He draws / anime
characters   in his sketchbook / on the days he doesn't / sleep   All self-
taught because   not once in / his four years here has his schedule
allowed / him to take an art elective   Another crack / he fell through
When class is over and he   /   wakes he apologizes   profusely   tells
me it isn't /   my fault I'm such / a good teacher   He gives his excuses
and I could add / on a pile of other reasons for his / slumping   body
but / none of that explains   the impossible distance he   crosses every
day / to be here   He is reaching across /   a growing fissure   sincere
in a way only   kids can be   I / feel him   tug at my heart   draw on
something like guilt or shame   a thing less / scalding but worse for
that And   then   I am reaching   back   across my own growing chasm
/   in the pockets of time where I'm not teaching feminist theory or
how to write a timed essay   not / reaching across other impossible
distances towards other drifting / students not batting down   banal
resentments   My knocks on the table   beside his head   must come
from / another universe   arriving /   as only faint   signals   a trick
of the   /   ear   perhaps

DISPATCH
re: Tea and Hot Chocolate

> *Tita was literally "like water for chocolate"–she was on the verge of boiling over. . . . She felt her head about to burst, like a kernel of popcorn.*
>   —Laura Esquivel

The path to my students' hearts / is through hot chocolate and sugar cubes for tea   We are all here / save one student / second period on Friday No / one can work / I / can't even pretend I refresh / refresh / refresh my email   the WESA / website for any news about / whether schools will close about / when How long does coronavirus stay alive on surfaces Most students / today across the building / are absent but this is AP Lit and these / kids are / safe and successful in school   The musical sponsors Ms. Jay and Mr. Cartwright have just / told them that the musical is indefinitely / on hold and anyways Mr. Cartwright got / a new job and he is leaving So we plug in the kettles / and listen to the slowly rising roar until bubbles / burst above the water's surface We stir powder / dunk tea bags   We Clorox wipe the tables and circle / up   I spread the Tea & Empathy   cards across the center table / Their now familiar emotions and three synonyms / pool beneath our fingertips The students   choose cards for how they feel / sip   from styrofoam / They choose cards for how they want to feel They feel anxious scared hopeless shitty They want to feel in control assured powerful hopeful   I feel   despondent unsettled my familiar rage / turning inside out I want to feel   helpful   I am only as helpful as my / sugar supply Nothing is canceled   yet But we all / sense that it is over   that this is all there is / left of this year So we stand in our / solemn little circle   swallow down what threatens to   boil over

DISPATCH
re: Intaglio

On the   third day of the stay-at-home order   / my finger itched badly / beneath my wedding   ring   I took it off and left it / off for days   longer / than I have ever gone   without   it   Even days / later   a recessed   band   banded / my ring finger   with love   In sculpture this is   / intaglio   a design cut   / into the surface   the opposite   / of relief   I haven't seen my students   in   two   / weeks   I haven't gone   /   so long   without students   since / my children were born   Even / summers   I   /   run   an online   discussion board with   / my AP Lit students   to keep them reading   / writing   engaged / with one another   The district told us   / do   nothing   Do nothing   for two weeks   /   Now that we are back   / on the clock   we still cannot   / grade   not even work submitted   before the / closure   If we reach out   /   be sure to use the approved   district language   /   if only they gave us   /   the language   an agenda   a memo   anything   They did   / not   they also do   no/thing   I   still feel   /   my students   through   their / fear   /   griefs they   can/not articulate   Their absence is   intaglio / a ligature   circling   my throat

DISPATCH
re: Quiet

When I was   breastfeeding my son   /   I spent many hours in the rocking chair in the nursery / in the middle of the night   This is not the point   my   hours in the chair   or the way I   punished myself / with breastfeeding   a child who   didn't love it like I wanted   him / to   The point is /   how quiet the world was at   3am   So quiet / I could hear the   excavators and the /   bulldozers working on the commercial drag a mile / from our home   In the green chair with the blue   nightlight On the moonlit asphalt we / were   alone but   together   working / in the middle of the night   Last night / not falling asleep   not falling asleep   the choice to   / not take that   Unisom   the quality   /   of silence was similar   But it was only   10 o'clock   The world was already   /   packed away tight for the night A train   whistled in the   far/off   I remember being young   /   maybe ten   and sleeping / in the room that is now my daughter's   hearing that same /   train whistle   I'm not / sleeping so well / again /   When I finally slept I   dreamt of /   teaching and Ms. Long   We were teaching inside /   a refrigerator together When she   /   removed the cheese drawer   we could see through the back of the fridge /   to a moist and distant cement   gutter where / our students   were / just barely visible   They were so / very far   /   from us

DISPATCH
re: Equity

I tell students / always at some point / there is no right time but I / feel it out as best I can that / I have no college debt because my parents paid for me Paid for me to / go to Johns Hopkins University and also really / paid for my graduate degree at Sarah Lawrence College These are names / that enter the room before I do and sometimes I try to / not talk about them Even though the school rules have me / post them on the bulletin board outside my door Every year someone asks if my parents / are interested in adopting / a high school senior from Frontier High School I understand / how I got where I am and they understand / they can't get there from here In the lockdown / we are all at home and my home is large with a large yard / our lives in this home are / easy The down payment was a gift of equity / a term I didn't know until my / parents taught it to me The longer I spend thinking about / how my life looks next to my students' the more / grief threatens to choke me Perhaps it's also / guilt Fixing the inequity means losing / these privileges Today in the shower I thought about / what the pandemic has torn open and felt / no hope at all of changing the world I can teach my students about Marxism and intersectional feminism I can teach / them to write big beefy arguments based on text evidence but teaching is / not a gift of equity

DISPATCH
re: the Sun

> *Everyone wants to be close to the sun. And you, the teacher, are the sun.*
> —Madeleine Ray

In New York City   the mayor and / the governor are in a pissing
match over who / has the authority to close the schools   Almost as
if /   the biggest problem was who   /   was losing to whom and not
that our / schools stand as the   final remaining knots of the social
/ safety net   In Pennsylvania our / schools are already closed for
the year but Philadelphia has / such poor   broadband connectivity
and the families so few   /   devices they aren't allowed to do much
beyond offer packets / optional lessons Frontier is proudly passing
out computers   We must have put / out a press release because
there we / were on all the local news channels But / I know there
is a long technology waiting list and / concern that the list is longer
than   the number of computers we still have Still students / show
up to the Google classroom There are no grades   I am not there
to put a hand on a shoulder or give / the stink eye In a pedagogy
book   I read once that   the teacher is the / sun   All the students
want to be near / her turn their faces to her / warmth Am I still
the sun while so   / far away   We are their teachers We /   are
the sun and they want   us to shine on them   even as our heat
is receding And this is what I asked for   isn't it   to burn out /
without smoking A dying sun   grows and grows turns red   until it
collapses on itself leaving behind a nebula of   gas and dust I feel
like   a cloud of gas and dust It's just I / just I never thought I
would   go /   out like this

DISPATCH
re: a Pause

There are two kinds of apple trees in / my neighborhood   For
years I would worry   that something / had killed the crabapple
blossoms on my childhood trees But now I know they / simply
blossom later than the nursery bought trees down the road The
nursery bought trees bloom cotton ball white / and early On my
trees a few weeks later and after / the green leaves unfurl   tight
magenta buds give way to / soft pink petals and sweet perfume
This year it has / been cold and I have watched snow fall on the
buds / I have panicked at / frost warnings in late April But still
every morning / the buds draw their coats tighter against the cold
/ and they seem / fine The trees have pressed / pause I think this
life in quarantine is what I've fantasized about /   for a while
now A life of the mind I read I write I / shower while thinking
deep thoughts But what is a life of the mind without / the students
to share it with It is a / pause a dream / where I smile / as my
teeth / fall out   and petal soft blankets / close all around me   a
question about / how long the closed bud persists

DISPATCH
re: Magical Realism

Your task is to   write a small poem / or story   based on the mundane
details from   your writer's diary   Include / ample sensory details
Then / after you finish   revise the piece   /   by transforming at least
one ordinary detail   into something   wild / magical

Today I   go back to my classroom to pack /   it all in for the year   I
do not pack   not / really   I have   so many video tutorials   to record
So many / Google Comments to leave on /   excellent work   on half-
assed work   Students /   to text   emojis to copy   and / paste   We
arrive / in   staggered shifts   two hours   each /   masks required
/ no one in the same /   hallway   I am   alone and   steaming / up
my   glasses   The furniture has already been shoved to the / center
of the room   Books are on the floor   fallen   from /   the   shelves
/   I take all my kids' artwork   / down from the walls   Emmett's
Abraham Lincoln with anime eyes   a picture by Willa   of me with
uncharacteristically   long /   legs and plaid pants   A drawing of an
alien by H. but / the alien really looks like a tentacled / vagina   the
wall of selfies   all those /   students in blue gowns   mortarboards /
and   shining smiles   I throw away the /   chart paper   anchor
charts   tracing the themes of / the year   fire   and   oppression   and
storytelling and history   Or is it   History   We could / never decide
Usually   I save /   student notebooks   until the end of fall   in case
they come / back   for them   But this year   I   throw composition
notebook   after   composition /   notebook into a giant   rolling
trashcan   They fall from / my hands and   swish   against the black
plastic liner   A truncated year's worth of   big / beefy paragraphs
of Cornell notes on   reader response theories   feminism   Marxism
/ psychoanalysis   From the trashcan comes a sound like   flames /

licking   But I   look and / see it is roots and a trunk cracking
/ growing   Up /   bursts   an apple tree   / its branches   lengthen
curve to the skylight   They blossom with   fluttering   pastel blooms
white blooms   cerise pink   blooms   on / fire   with life   The
blossoms   /   shrivel   push forth   tiny apples   that grow larger
larger /   bending the branches with their   sweetness / I pluck
one and hold it /   to my lips   bite through   the tender /   skin   An
apple   crisp and / bright   with knowledge

DISPATCH
re: How we scatter

> *come to share our worlds witchu*
> *we come here to be dancin*
> *to be dancin*
> *to be dancin*
> *baya*
>   —Ntozake Shange

On   my way to a job interview /   at a / good / suburban school
I drove up /   the winding hill to the high school /   choking back
tears All along the drive /   the district has posted yard signs for
their /   seniors   Each senior / every one / has a personalized yard
sign with /   their name and   their senior portrait   Their hopeful
fall faces   standing in absentia   under the   lush   early summer
green Last night /   the teachers and administrators of my kids'
school district   drove in /   car parades   honking and screaming
and trailing streamers behind them through all / the neighborhoods
of the district   You Matter   our elementary school principal had
chalk-markered across   / her back windshield And /   I cried   and
cried   We have done /   nothing for our seniors   We have been
instructed   /   to do nothing We plot /   otherwise   We plot / to
bring   worlds to front doors   We create grab bags of goodies   /
Kool-Aid and /   cookies and finger puppets and invitations / to the
senior celebration Zoom My own kids /   helped me make dozens of
copies of my smiling face   cut out / and glued on a stick so / these
seniors can still   have a /   graduation selfie with Ms. Beddow for the
selfie wall   We meet in the school   parking lot   out by the Giant
Eagle / so no administrator will stop us   We finalize /   our routes
load / the treat boxes into trunks We take a ridiculous picture where

everyone is masked   / and half of us have sun glasses on but we know / how hard we are smiling We / dance for another picture swing our heads   push our legs /   to the sun We are too close but it is only for a /   moment And then   /   we scatter

NOTES

This book is in conversation with the stories, novels, poems, and other texts I shared with the students in my classroom. These texts helped me understand my identity as a teacher, a mentor, a friend, a woman, and a person striving for connection. The book returns again and again specifically to Ntozake Shange's *For colored girls who have considered suicide/when the rainbow is enuf: a choreopoem*, which I first read when I was a high school senior and which has served as an emotional touchstone for me ever since.

Dispatch re: You: This poem is in conversation with Giovanni Verga's "The Wolf" (translated by Alfred Alexander).

Dispatch re: Hope: The tweet referenced in this poem was once pinned to Eunsong Kim's Twitter (twitter.com/clepsydras) but has since been deleted.

Dispatch re: Monday's Bomb Threat: This poem is in conversation with Philip Larkin's poem "Toads."

Dispatch re: Beyoncé: This poem is in conversation with Beyoncé's "Formation."

Dispatch re: Labor: This poem is in conversation with Margaret Atwood's *The Handmaid's Tale.*

Dispatch re: my Love: This poem is in conversation with Ntozake Shange's "no more love poems #4," from *For colored girls.*

Dispatch re: End of Year Party: This poem is in conversation with Ta-Nehisi Coates' *Between the World and Me*.

Dispatch re: Satan at Our Backs: This poem is in conversation with Ntozake Shange's "a layin on of hands" and "sorry," both from *For colored girls*. The lines "I love them   on purpose   I am / open   on purpose" are very close paraphrases of lines from "sorry."

Dispatch re: Car Speakers: This poem is in conversation with "Venus Fly" by Grimes and Janelle Monáe. The line "tell all yr secrets bout yourself to yr face" is from Ntozake Shange's "sorry," in *For colored girls*.

Dispatch re: Gratitude: The phrase "hunkers like hard luck" comes from Philip Larkin's poem "Toads."

Dispatch re: Sex Dream: The comic referenced in the poem is David Heatley's "Portrait of My Dad: True Life Comic Vignettes."

Dispatch re: Paolo Freire: This poem is in conversation with Paolo Freire's *Pedagogy of the Oppressed* (translated by Myra Bergman Ramos).

Dispatch re: Potluck Love: The Tea & Empathy cards, as well as the exercise where the students choose cards for how they think someone else feels and wants to feel, were created by Kate Kenfield. Learn more at katekenfield.com. Order your own deck at teaandempathy.org.

Dispatch re: the Bud: This poem is in conversation with Galway Kinnell's "Saint Francis and the Sow."

Dispatch re: If/Then: The word "blueblack" is Robert Hayden's, from his poem "Those Winter Sundays." The "banked fire" in the poem is also a nod to Hayden.

Dispatch re: Safety on the Boulevard: This poem is in conversation with Elizabeth Bishop's "One Art."

Dispatch re: my Feminine Wiles: This poem is in conversation with Ntozake Shange's "somebody almost walked off wid alla my stuff," from *For colored girls.*

Dispatch re: All may be well: This poem is in conversation with William Shakespeare's *The Tragedy of Hamlet, Prince of Denmark.*

Dispatch re: I'm so sorry: This poem is in conversation with Ntozake Shange's "sorry," from *For colored girls.*

Dispatch to: Leah: This poem is in conversation with "Out of Touch," by Daryl Hall and John Oates.

Dispatch re: Out of joint: This poem is in conversation with Shakespeare's *Hamlet.*

Dispatch re: Tea and Hot Chocolate: The epigraph comes from Laura Esquivel's *Like Water for Chocolate.*

Dispatch re: the Sun: The epigraph comes from Madeleine Ray, as quoted in Ariel Sacks' *Whole Novels for the Whole Class.*

Dispatch re: How we scatter: This poem is in conversation with Ntozake Shange's "i'm a poet who," from *For colored girls.*

ACKNOWLEDGMENTS

"Dispatch re: Gratitude," "re: Stabbing Potatoes," and "re: Darkness" previously appeared in *Bone Bouquet*

"Dispatch re: Biblical Plagues" and "re: the Blossom of Youth" previously appeared in *Cotton Xenomorph*

"Dispatch re: Magical Realism" previously appeared in *Dream Pop Press*

"Dispatch re: We mustn't dwell, no not today" and "re: End of Year Party" previously appeared in *Ethel*

"Dispatch re: White Out" and "re: Intaglio" previously appeared in *Everything in Aspic*

"Dispatch re: Gun Day," "re: Childline," "re: Pink," and "from: the Bathroom" previously appeared in *GlitterMOB*

"Dispatch re: Ice in April," "re: Car Speakers," and "re: Big Dick" previously appeared in *Menacing Hedge*

"Dispatch for: [redacted]" and "to: Leah" previously appeared in *Night Music Journal*

"Dispatch re: my Teeth" previously appeared in *Stirring: A Literary Collection*

"Dispatch for: Colin Kaepernick" previously appeared in *TAB*

"Dispatch re: a Pause" and "re: Shadows" previously appeared in *Willawaw*

THANKS

Thank you to all the teachers, counselors, and staff I worked with at the real-life Frontier Schools. I learned so much from all of you about teaching, professionalism, and, most of all, love. I am a better teacher and a better person because of your invaluable lessons. Thank you most especially to Kharma (first work-wife of my heart), Elise, Max, Katey, Maggie, Chelsea, Kristen and Matt. Thank you also to Daphne and Adam, who were baby teachers with me in the Bronx.

Thank you to my teachers, from high school to grad school, who gave me such wisdom, love, and care. Most especially thank you to Terri Klein, Greg Williamson, Suzanne Gardinier, Kate Knapp Johnson, and Saul Brodsky.

Thank you to Courtney LeBlanc for believing in these poems and giving them a home at Riot in Your Throat. Thank you to the editors of *Bone Bouquet, Cotton Xenomorph, Dream Pop Press, Ethel zine, Everything in Aspic, GlitterMOB, Menacing Hedge, Night Music Journal, Stirring: A Literary Collection, TAB,* and *Willawaw* for giving many of these poems good homes.

Thank you to my husband Jeff, who has read more of my words than anyone on this planet and without whom our whole household would fall to pieces—without whom I would fall to pieces.

Thank you to Sarah Kain Gutowski who generously read an early version of this manuscript and provided me with thoughtful feedback and the kind of full-throated support I only ever expect from my parents. Thank you to Margaret Bashaar whose excitement, encouragement and expert advice helped me ground me as I looked for a home for this book. Thank you to Krystal Languell, Kelly Boyker, and Eunsong Kim for always lending me support and moral fortitude.

Thank you to my students. Thank you especially to Corinne, Hassan, Nsai, Suzen, and Kallie who read this book when it was only a PDF and offered so much love and support for me and the project.

Thank you to the members of the Poetry Cleanse group, who read so very many of these poems in their earliest forms and sent notes of praise, encouragement, and commiseration. Thank you to my Zoom writing group, without whom this pandemic would have been unbearable.

Thank you to everyone who read the very first poems in this book when I posted them in desperation on Facebook. Every one of your likes, hearts, and comments helped me feel less alone and less hopeless.

Thank you to my parents and parents-in-law and kids and siblings for always loving me.

Thank you to my blurbers, who volunteered their time and words to support this book: Rachel Mennies, Krystal Languell, and Sarah Kain Gutowski. I so admire all of your poetry and all of your work in this world, and your endorsements mean the world to me.

ABOUT THE AUTHOR

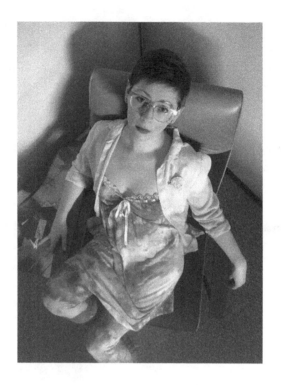

Sarah Beddow is a poet, wife and mother. She is the author of the book *Dispatches from Frontier Schools* (Riot in Your Throat) and the chapbook *What's pink & shiny / what's dark and hard* (Porkbelly Press). Her poems and essays have appeared in *Bone Bouquet, Menacing Hedge, Entropy, GlitterMOB,* and elsewhere. She has degrees in creative writing from Johns Hopkins University and Sarah Lawrence College. After completing her MFA in poetry, she earned an MS in Urban Education from Mercy College and spent nearly a decade teaching high school English. Though she now works in educational publishing, she looks forward to one day returning to the classroom.

ABOUT THE PRESS

Riot in Your Throat is an independent press
that publishes fierce, feminist poetry.

Support independent authors, artists, and presses.

Visit us online:
www.riotinyourthroat.com

CPSIA information can be obtained
at www.ICGtesting.com
Printed in the USA
JSHW021433080722
27704JS00004B/22